T H R O U [G H]

THE EYES
OF THE CREE
AND BEYOND

THE ART OF ALLEN SAPP: THE STORY OF A PEOPLE

Dean Bauche, Curator/conservateur

Lyndon Tootoosis, Curator/conservateur

Lorne Carrier, Curator/conservateur

With Essays by/avec des essais de

D. G. Bauche, L. Whiteman, L. Carrier, D. Musqua

ALLEN SAPP GALLERY
THE GONOR COLLECTION

www.allensapp.com

THROUGH THE EYES OF THE CREE AND BEYOND
– The Art of Allen Sapp: The Story of a People

First Printing, February 2005

Published by
Allen Sapp Gallery
1 Railway Avenue East
P.O. Box 460
North Battleford, Saskatchewan, Canada S9A 2Y6

The Allen Sapp Gallery is a public gallery supported by membership and owned and funded by the City of North Battleford and the Province of Saskatchewan.

This exhibition has been organized and circulated by the Allen Sapp Gallery with the support of many people.

Front Cover: **Late for the Meeting**, Allen Sapp, 1972

Library and Archives Canada Cataloguing in Publication

Sapp Allen, 1929-

Through the eyes of the Cree and beyond : the art of Allen Sapp : the story of a people / editor/coordinator, Dean Bauche.
Includes text in English, French and Cree.
Catalogue of an exhibition opening in North Battleford in the fall of 2004 and travelling to 9 other museums during 2005.

ISBN 1-897010-14-1 (bound) – ISBN 1-897010-13-3 (pbk.)

1. Sapp, Allen, 1929 – Exhibitions. 2. Elders (Native peoples) – Prairie Provinces.
3. Cree Indians – Prairie Provinces – History. 4. Indians of North America – Prairie Provinces – History.
I. Bauche, Dean, 1955- II. Allen Sapp Gallery III. Title.

ND249.S25A4 2005   759.11   C2005-901051-7

Cover and page design by
Brian Danchuk, Brian Danchuk Design

Formatting by
Iona Glabus, Centax Books

Printed and Produced in Canada by
Centax Books, a division of PrintWest Communications Ltd.
Publishing Director and Editor – Margo Embury
1150 Eighth Avenue, Regina, Saskatchewan, Canada S4R 1C9
(306) 525-2304   Fax (306) 757-2439
E-mail: centax@printwest.com   www.centaxbooks.com

TABLE OF CONTENTS

ACKNOWLEDGEMENTS

The Allen Sapp Gallery gratefully acknowledges the financial investment by the Department of Canadian Heritage, the Province of Saskatchewan, the Office of the Treaty Commissioner, and the City of North Battleford in the creation of this national touring exhibition.

We would like to thank the following participants for their hard work and dedication to this project:

Elders
Allen and Margaret Sapp, Red Pheasant First Nation
Edwin Tootoosis, Poundmaker First Nation
Bernice and Wallace Simaganis, Poundmaker First Nation
Jonas Semaganis, Little Pine First Nation
Josephine Frank, Poundmaker First Nation
Simon Sapp, Little Pine First Nation
Irene Fineday, Sweetgrass First Nation
Danny Musqua, Keeseekoose First Nation, Anishinabe
 (Saulteaux) Nation
William Stone, Mosquito First Nation, Nakota
 (Assiniboine) Nation
Solomon Stone, Mosquito First Nation, Nakota
 (Assiniboine) Nation
Melvina Eagle, Whitecap Dakota Sioux First Nation,
 Dakota (Sioux) Nation
Dolly Neapetung, Yellow Quill First Nation, Anishinabe
 (Saulteaux)Nation
Alma Kytwayhat, Makwa Sahgaiehcan First Nation
Lloyd and Noreen Howe, Cut Knife

City of North Battleford

Allen Sapp Gallery
Dean Bauche: Director/Design
Kathy Dill – Technical Support
Roger Giesbrecht – photography
Robin Dyck
Angela Edmunds
Ruby Klassen
Claudette McGuire

Project Management
Eclear Consulting
Elements
 Leah Garven
 Al Dyck

Cultural Consultants
Wes Fineday
Lyndon Tootoosis
Joseph Naytowhow
Ken Fineday
Dwayne Sapp

Curators
Dean Bauche
Lyndon Tootoosis
Lorne Carrier

Artifacts on Loan from:
Royal Saskatchewan Museum
Gordon Angus
Neil Dyck
Wes Fineday
Simon Sapp
Doyle Tootoosis
Kenneth Tootoosis
Lyndon Tootoosis
Saskatchewan Arts Board
The collection of the Glenbow Museum, Calgary, Alberta

Video Narration
Dean Bauche – Writer
Gordon Tootoosis – English

Editing
John Srayko
Jamie Bauche

Design Layout
Dean Bauche
Kathy Dill
Leah Garven

Editorial
Lori Whiteman
Lorne Carrier
Danny Musqua
Dean Bauche

Catalogue Translation and Proofing
Patricia Leguen – French
Arok Wolvengrey – Cree
Jean Okimâsis – Cree

ACKNOWLEDGEMENTS

Support
Jean Claude Horel
Kelly's Computer Works
Menno Fieguth Photography

MGM
Debra Piapot
Paul O'Byrne

Department of Canadian Heritage

Saskatchewan Centennial 2005

Royal Saskatchewan Museum

Office of the Treaty Commissioner
Alma Kytwayhat
Danny Musqua
David Arnot
Bev Kynoch
Kay Lerat
Darrell Seib

Teacher Resource Guide Contributors
Bev Kynoch, Curriculum Writer
  Office of the Treaty Commissioner

Northwest Catholic School Division
Herb Sutton
Carol Oake
Sheldon Revet

Battlefords School Division
Tammy Haugen
Patty Serwotski
Anne Marie Merle

Sweetgrass First Nation School
Brenda Albert
Elizabeth Lechance
Walter Korolchuk

Students
Alex Dreaver
Hadassaha Flamond
James Fisher
Shayleen Isaac

Saskatchewan Valley School Division
Maxine Gamble

Web Site Translation
Arok Wolvengrey – Cree
Jean Okimâsis – Cree
Dwayne Sapp – Cree
Ken Fineday – Cree
Liz Myo – Cree
Bernard Millette – French
Linda Michaud – French
Leanne Merkowsky – French

ECS Energy, Calculations & Solutions Inc.
Bernard Millette – French
Leanne Merkowsky – French

***miywâsin* ink**
Arok Wolvengrey – Cree
Jean Okimâsis – Cree

Production
Access Communications
  (formerly Battlefords Community Cablevision)
MerJak Multimedia and Consulting
Chris Bajak
Haley Kalous

Cultural Advisors
Alma Kytwayhat, Makwa Sahgaiehcan First Nation
Wes Fineday, Sweetgrass First Nation
Lyle Trottier, Onion Lake First Nation

Saskatoon Public School Division
Diane Okrainetz
W Neil Pechey
Alison Uitti
Tamara Chief

Saskatoon Catholic School Division
Anna Leah King

Sakewew High School
Lorraine Standing Water
Louise Bear

**Willow Cree Education Complex
Beardy's and Okemasis First Nation**
Anita Cameron

Canadian Heritage **Patrimoine canadien**

Greetings to all those taking part in the journey: *Through the Eyes of the Cree and Beyond* exhibition.

It is important for all peoples to preserve and promote their culture and way of life. This is particularly true of Aboriginal peoples in Canada, whose cultures form the foundation of our appreciation of diversity and continue to enrich our common heritage. *Through the Eyes of the Cree and Beyond* uses digital technology to bring Cree traditions and lifestyle to life through the reminiscences of those who have helped preserve them and the brilliant art of Allen Sapp.

As Minister of Canadian Heritage, I am pleased to support this unique exhibition that provides all Canadians with an insight into Aboriginal culture.

Enjoy the Exhibition!

J'aimerais souhaiter la bienvenue à tous ceux et celles qui prennent part à ce voyage : l'exposition *À travers les regards des Cris et au-delà*.

Il est important pour tous les peuples de pouvoir préserver leur culture et leur mode de vie. Cela est d'autant plus vrai pour les Autochtones au Canada, dont les cultures sont la fondation de notre appréciation de la diversité et continuent à enrichir notre patrimoine commun. *À travers les regards des Cris et au-delà* utilise la technologie numérique pour faire revivre les coutumes et les traditions cries grâce aux récits de ceux qui les ont perpétuées et au génie artistique d'Allen Sapp.

À titre de ministre du Patrimoine canadien, je suis ravie d'appuyer cette exposition unique en son genre qui représente pour tous les Canadiens et Canadiennes une fenêtre ouverte sur la culture autochtone.

Bonne exposition!

Liza Frulla

Canada

MESSAGE FROM THE TREATY COMMISSIONER

As Treaty Commissioner for Saskatchewan, I have had the honour and privilege of spending a considerable amount of time working with and learning from Treaty Elders over the past several years. Their wisdom, knowledge and memories serve their people well in preserving and transmitting First Nations history, treaty knowledge and cultural practices to younger generations.

This catalogue and the exhibition of Allen Sapp's art, *Through the Eyes of the Cree and Beyond*, captures the history, knowledge and memories of Cree Elders as well as Elders representing other Plains First Nations peoples. Through Sapp's art and through the eyes of the Elders, an important era in the history of First Nations people in Canada is captured and presented for all people to experience.

Enjoy the exhibition!

Honourable Judge David Arnot
Treaty Commissioner for Saskatchewan

En tant que Commissaire aux traités de la Saskatchewan, j'ai eu l'honneur et le privilège au cours des dernières années de passer énormément de temps à travailler avec les Aînés de l'époque des traités et ils m'ont beaucoup appris. Leur sagesse, leurs connaissances et leurs souvenirs ont bien servi leur peuple en préservant l'histoire des Premières nations, les connaissances concernant les traités et les pratiques culturelles et en les transmettant aux générations plus jeunes.

Ce catalogue et cette exposition de tableaux d'Allen Sapp *À travers les regards des Cris et au-delà* présentent l'histoire, les connaissances et les souvenirs des Aînés cris et aussi d'autres Aînés représentant d'autres Premières nations des Plaines. À travers l'art d'Allen Sapp et à travers les regards des Aînés, une ère importante de l'histoire des Premières nations du Canada est présentée pour que tout le monde en prenne connaissance.

Bonne exposition!

L'honorable juge David Arnot
Commissaire aux traités de la Saskatchewan

MESSAGE FROM THE SASKATCHEWAN CENTENNIAL 2005 CHAIR

As Saskatchewan celebrates its centennial year, we are honoured to support *Through the Eyes of the Cree and Beyond*. This multimedia exhibition combines the artwork of Allen Sapp with the voices of Elders and youth to describe the rich past of Northern Plains Cree and their aspirations for the future. The exhibition bridges cultures and connects communities, providing opportunity to discover the many common experiences that we share. It is an exhibition that will teach, inform, challenge and entertain.

Saskatchewan is proud to be home to Allen Sapp, an artist whose work is world renowned. I congratulate everyone involved with *Through the Eyes of the Cree and Beyond*. Your dedication to this project has created a meaningful legacy that captures an important part of our past, present and future.

Enjoy!

Glenn Hagel, MLA
Chair, Saskatchewan Centennial 2005

Alors que la Saskatchewan célèbre son centenaire, c'est un honneur pour nous d'appuyer *À travers les regards des Cris et au-delà*. Cette exposition multimédia associe l'œuvre d'Allen Sapp aux voix d'Aînés et de jeunes pour décrire le riche passé des Cris des Plaines du Nord et leurs aspirations face à l'avenir. Cette exposition rapproche les cultures et unit les communautés en offrant la possibilité de découvrir les nombreuses expériences communes que nous partageons. C'est une exposition qui saura enseigner, informer, stimuler et divertir.

La Saskatchewan est fière de compter parmi les siens Allen Sapp, un artiste dont l'œuvre est de renommée internationale. Je félicite tous ceux et toutes celles qui ont participé au projet *À travers les regards de Cris et au-delà*. Votre dévouement envers ce projet a créé un legs précieux qui reflète une partie importante de notre passé, de notre présent et de notre avenir.

Bonne visite!

Glenn Hagel, député provincial
Président du Centenaire 2005 de la Saskatchewan

A TEAM APPROACH

The curators selected the art, artifacts and photography in this catalogue after extensive team consultation. Elders Jonas Semaganis, Irene Fineday and the Office of the Treaty Commissioner staff were a part of that team process. Wes Fineday was the key consultant in developing the commentary and painting themes which offer a First Nations perspective on the art of Allen Sapp.

Curators

Dean Bauche – Curator of art and digital production, Director/Curator of the Allen Sapp Gallery since its inception in 1989; main architect of the Virtual Museum of Canada project *Through the Eyes of the Cree*.

Lorne Carrier – Artifact curator, works as Museums Association of Saskatchewan Community Development Manager; previous curator of Treaty Four Keeping House and Archives; First Nations Liaison Officer; Interpreter Wanuskewin Heritage Park.

Lyndon Tootoosis – Curator of photography/historical research, Gallery staff and native cultural liaison/consultant for Allen Sapp Gallery; previous Director of Poundmaker Interpretive Centre.

First Nations Consultant

Wes Fineday has worked as a consultant for the Allen Sapp Gallery since its inception in 1989. He has also worked as a consultant for Wanuskewin Heritage Park, Justice Canada, Gabriel Dumont Institute, and the University of Saskatchewan. His knowledge of First Nations history, law, philosophy, and spirituality are truly remarkable. All of his knowledge is based on extensive consultation and time spent with respected First Nations Elders of Saskatchewan and beyond.

Essayists

Dr. Danny Musqua – Saulteaux from the Keeseekoose First Nation, Elder Musqua has worked as a Communication Officer with the Federation of Saskatchewan Indian Nations, as resident Elder with the College of Education, University of Saskatchewan, and as an associate professor at the First Nations University of Canada. Elder Musqua was presented with a Doctorate of Laws by the University of Saskatchewan because of his impact in the area of Traditional Teachings and Methodologies of First Nations' world views.

Laura (Lori) Whiteman – Dakota/Saulteaux and band member of the Standing Buffalo Dakota First Nation, Lori is the Education Equity Consultant with the Regina Public School Division. A teacher, she has also worked as an adult-education and youth-life-skills facilitator. She feels a responsibility to our future generations, to ensure that past mistakes are not repeated and that the beauty of First Nations cultures is shared in a positive way.

UNE APPROCHE D'ÉQUIPE

Les conservateurs ont sélectionné les œuvres, les artefacts et les photos qui se trouvent dans ce catalogue après de longues consultations avec l'équipe. Les Aînés Jonas Semaganis et Irene Fineday et le personnel du bureau du commissaire aux traités ont participé à ce processus de collaboration. Wes Fineday a été le principal conseiller dans le développement du commentaire et des thèmes des tableaux qui offrent une perspective des Premières nations sur l'art d'Allen Sapp.

Conservateurs

Dean Bauche – Conservateur d'art et de production numérique, directeur et conservateur de la galerie Allen Sapp depuis sa création en 1989; principal architecte du projet du Musée virtuel du Canada intitulé *À travers les regards des Cris*.

Lorne Carrier – Conservateur d'artefacts, travaille comme gérant du développement communautaire de la Museums Association of Saskatchewan; conservateur à Treaty Four Keeping House and Archives; agent de liaison des Premières nations; interprète au parc du patrimoine Wanuskewin.

Lyndon Tootoosis – Conservateur en photographie et recherche historique, employé de la galerie, conseiller culturel autochtone et personne liaison pour la galerie Allen Sapp; ancien directeur du Poundmaker Interpretive Centre.

Conseiller des Premières nations

Wes Fineday travaille comme conseiller pour la galerie Allen Sapp depuis sa création en 1989. Wes a aussi travaillé comme conseiller pour le parc du patrimoine Wanuskewin, pour le ministère de la Justice du Canada, pour le Gabriel Dumont Institute et pour l'Université de la Saskatchewan. Ses connaissances sur l'histoire, le droit, la philosophie et la spiritualité des Premières nations sont vraiment remarquables. Toutes ses connaissances sont basées sur des consultations élaborées et du temps passé avec des Aînés respectés des Premières nations de la Saskatchewan et d'ailleurs.

Essayistes

Danny Musqua LL. D. – Saulteaux de la Première nation Keeseekoose, située dans la région de Kamsack-Yorkton. L'Aîné Musqua a travaillé comme agent de communication à la Fédération des nations indiennes de la Saskatchewan, comme Aîné en poste au collège d'éducation de l'Université de la Saskatchewan et comme professeur adjoint à l'Université des Premières nations du Canada. L'Aîné Musqua a reçu un doctorat en droit du collège d'éducation de l'Université de la Saskatchewan. Cette distinction lui a été décernée en raison de son impact dans le domaine des enseignements traditionnels et des méthodologies de la vision du monde des Premières nations.

Laura (Lori) Whiteman – Dakota/Saulteaux et membre de la bande de la Première nation Dakota Standing Buffalo, Lori est actuellement conseillère pour l'équité en matière d'éducation à la division des écoles publiques de Regina. Elle a été enseignante et elle a aussi travaillé comme animatrice en éducation pour adultes et en aptitudes à la vie quotidienne pour les jeunes. En tant qu'éducatrice, elle pense qu'elle a une responsabilité énorme envers les futures générations. Elle veut s'assurer que les erreurs du passé ne se répèteront pas et que la beauté des cultures des Premières nations sera partagée d'une manière positive.

"I paint because I like to paint, not because people pay money for my work. Money, we need it but it is people who are more important."
– *Allen Sapp*

"Je peins parce que j'aime peindre, pas parce que le gens me paient pour mon travail. L'argent, nous en avons besoin mais ce sont les gens qui sont plus importants."
– *Allen Sapp*

ELDER CONTRIBUTORS

Danny Musqua

Edwin Tootoosis

Jonas Semaganis

Simon Sapp

Wallace Simaganis

Solomon Stone

Alma Kytwayhat

Bernice Simaganis

Dolly Neapetung

Irene Fineday

Gordon Tootoosis

Josephine Frank

It could be said that Allen Sapp has been gifted as keeper of the story through images. His story has been given added dimension and new meaning through the rich commentaries and reflections offered by the diverse group of Elders who have graciously contributed to this project.

Nous pouvons dire qu'Allen Sapp a reçu le don de gardien de l'histoire par le biais des images. Les riches commentaires et réflexions qui ont été offerts de bonne grâce par le groupe varié d'Aînés qui ont contribué à ce projet ont donné à son histoire une autre dimension et une nouvelle signification.

BRIDGING PAST TO PRESENT

Despite much bitterness and sadness, there is joy in the richness of the values of the Plains Cree culture. The need to reclaim this history, to be assured that our Ancestors' ways of knowing and living have not been forgotten, allows the generation of today to build, from history, a rich future. Allen's paintings bear witness to a past that held none of the distorted misperceptions and stereotypes that have led to layers of shame. Through these paintings, and with the support of the Elders, we can reconstruct an honourable history that will carry this, and future generations, forward with dignity. Each painting is an anchor that bridges past to present to future.

Excerpt from the essay *Through the Eyes of the Cree*
Lori Whiteman and Lorne Carrier

RELIER LE PASSÉ AU PRÉSENT

En dépit de beaucoup d'amertume et de tristesse, la culture des Cris des Plaines comporte de la joie dans la richesse de ses valeurs. Le besoin de reconquérir cette histoire, de s'assurer que les connaissances et la façon de vivre de nos ancêtres ne seront pas oubliées, permet à la génération d'aujourd'hui de développer, à partir de l'histoire, un avenir riche. Les tableaux d'Allen témoigne d'un passé où les idées fausses et les stéréotypes qui ont abouti à des couches successives de honte n'existaient pas. Grâce à ces tableaux et avec l'appui des Aînés nous pouvons reconstituer une histoire honorable qui permettra à la génération actuelle et aux générations futures d'aller de l'avant avec dignité. Chaque peinture est un point d'ancrage qui relie le passé au présent et au futur.

Extrait de l'essai *À travers les regards des Cris*
Lori Whiteman et Lorne Carrier

Ê-ÂNISKOTASTÂHK KAYÂS KÎKWAY ASICI ANOHC KÎKWAY

âta mistahi ê-ihtakok pîkwêyihtamowin mîna pîkiskâtamowin kêyâpic miyawâtamowin ihtakon mîna anima kâ-wêyôtahk paskwâwi-nêhiyaw isîhcikêwin kêyâpic. tâpwê piko ta-wâyinîtotamihk kayâs kîkway êkosi ka-isi-kêhcinâhohk êkâ ta-wanihkêhk tânisi kitayisiyiniminawak ê-kî-isi-waskawîtotahkik opimâtisiwiniwâw ayis anima êwako kita-kî-wîcihikowak ôki oski-nêhiyawak ôtê pêci-nîkân. namôya kîkway ta-nêpêwihikohk êkota nôkwan otâpasinahikêwinihk awa *Allen* âta mâna ê-kî-tâpwêhtamihk maci-kîkway ê-is-âyâcik iyiniwak. mâka nawac ôtê nîkân âniskotâpânak ka-kiskêyihtamwak wâpahtahkwâwi anita tâpasinahikêwinihk mîna ka-wîcihikwak kêhtê-aya ta-kiskisicik iyikohk ê-kî-kistêyihtâkosicik iyiniwak êkwa wiyawâw ta-mamihcêyimâcik otâniskê-ohtâwîwâwa. pâh-pêyak ôhi tâpasinahikêwina êkota ê-wâpahcikâtêk tânisi ka-kî-âniskômakahk kayâs kîkway asici anohc mîna ôtê nîkân kîkway.

"nêhiyaw kâ-isi-wâpahtahk" masinahikêwinisihk ôma ohci
Lori Whiteman and Lorne Carrier

ALLEN SAPP: HIS STORY

"Then one night I had a dream, I dreamed of houses, many houses. I dreamed I saw one tall building which had an opening. There he (Allen) stood in broad daylight. I spoke of my dream to others long ago. It frightened me. This must have been what I dreamed about, where he stands today."
– Alex Sapp

Alex Sapp, Allen Sapp's father, died in 1992 at the age of 91. In the 1970s he shared this dream with Thecla Bradshaw, who at the time was working on the first book on the life of Allen Sapp. Even then it had become apparent to many, including Allen's own father, that Allen was emerging as one of Canada's pre-eminent painters.

Allen Sapp was born in the winter of 1928 on the Red Pheasant Reserve in north-central Saskatchewan. He was a weak and sickly child, born to a mother who also suffered from illness and eventually died of tuberculosis while Allen was away at residential school. Allen was raised and cared for by Maggie Soonias, his maternal grandmother. The memory of this tender relationship has spawned in Sapp some of his finest and most sensitive works.

Allen never learned to read or write but found refuge and satisfaction in drawing pictures. When he was eight years old and suffering again from a childhood illness, his grandmother's sister Nootokao (*nôtokêw*, the old woman) had a dream in which she saw Allen threatened seriously with death. This dream compelled her to bestow a Cree name upon Allen. She touched his forehead as he slept and called him Kiskayetum (*kiskêyihtam*, He perceives it).

As Allen grew older he developed his gifts and found great satisfaction in painting and drawing. At the age of fourteen he was stricken with spinal meningitis. The recovery from this near-fatal illness was slow and exhausting. Nootokao had promised he would not succumb to illness but live to make Nehiyawak (*nêhiyawak*, the Cree people) proud of him and become a blessing to both Nehiyawak and the white race.

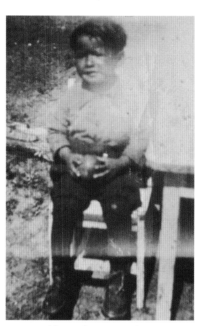

Allen at three years of age
Allen à l'âge de trois ans

ALLEN SAPP : SON HISTOIRE

"Puis une nuit j'ai fait un rêve ; j'ai rêvé de maisons, beaucoup de maisons. J'ai rêvé que je voyais un grand édifice qui avait une ouverture. (Allen) Il était debout là en plein jour. J'ai raconté ce rêve à d'autres personnes il y a longtemps. Il m'a effrayé ce rêve. C'est à ça que j'ai dû rêvé, où il se trouve aujourd'hui."
– Alex Sapp

Alex Sapp, le père d'Allen, est mort en 1994 à l'âge de 92 ans. Dans les années 1970 il raconta ce rêve à Thecla Bradshaw, qui à l'époque préparait le premier livre sur la vie d'Allen Sapp. Beaucoup de personnes, y compris le père d'Allen, avaient déjà réalisé qu'Allen se révélait comme un des peintres canadiens prééminents.

Allen Sapp est né au cours de l'hiver 1928 à la réserve Red Pheasant, dans le centre-nord de la Saskatchewan. C'était un enfant chétif et maladif né d'une mère malade aussi, qui par la suite mourut de la tuberculose quand Allen était au pensionnat. Allen a été élevé par Maggie Soonias, sa grand-mère maternelle. Le souvenir de cette relation pleine de tendresse a produit chez Sapp des œuvres qui sont parmi les plus touchantes et les plus belles.

Allen n'a jamais appris à lire ou à écrire mais il trouvait refuge et satisfaction dans le dessin. Quand il avait huit ans et qu'il souffrait encore d'une maladie infantile, la sœur de sa grand-mère – Nootokao (*nôtokêw*, la vieille femme) fit un rêve dans lequel elle vit que la mort menaçait sérieusement Allen. Ce rêve la poussa à donner un nom cri à Allen. Elle lui toucha le front pendant son sommeil et l'appela Kiskayetum (*kiskêyihtam*, Il le perçoit).

En grandissant, les dons d'Allen se développèrent et le dessin et la peinture lui apportaient une grande satisfaction. À l'âge de 14 ans, il fut atteint d'une méningite spinale. La convalescence qui suivit cette maladie quasi fatale fut lente et épuisante. Nootokao avait promis qu'il ne succomberait pas à la maladie mais qu'il vivrait pour que Nehiyawak (*nêhiyawak*, le peuple cri) soit fier de lui et qu'il devienne une bénédiction à la fois pour Nehiyawak et pour la race blanche.

There was a purpose for this frail one who made such a determined effort to live. One day he would be instrumental in communicating to the world his own humble story with an honesty and clarity that would be held as an expression of a larger story, that of his own people, the Northern Plains Cree.

Today Allen Sapp's canvases, more than those of any other Canadian artist, centre on family and community. Even when a canvas does not contain a single person, its title or content alludes to the presence of individuals who make up an intimate part of its memory. For thousands of years community and survival had gone hand in hand for Allen's people. His grandparents were part of the last generation to live the nomadic hunting life and of the first to make the transition to treaties and reserve life. Their sense of community had been intensified by a new imperative: survival in the face of the annihilation of the buffalo, westward expansion and government restrictions aimed at cultural assimilation.

Allen was steeped in the world view shared by his grandparents and those of their generation. They held that the land, family, spirituality and community are all intimately connected and his art testifies to this. The traditional world view Allen knew as a child held that generosity was integral to happiness and, indeed, survival. An individual giftedness or talent was a "spiritual blessing" to be shared with family as well as with the larger community.

"The artist is considered spiritually gifted for the common good of the community."
– Bob Boyer

This may help explain the strong sense of community expressed in Sapp's art. More importantly, it also explains why so many of his people connect strongly with Sapp's paintings, claiming Sapp's story as their own – belonging to them and indeed, their grandchildren. They see his

People Visiting Inside
Personnes en visite à l'interieur

Il y avait une raison d'être pour ce frêle adolescent qui avait lutté de façon si déterminée pour rester en vie. Un jour, il jouerait un rôle déterminant pour communiquer au monde son humble histoire avec une honnêteté et une clarté telles qu'on les considérerait comme l'expression d'une plus grande histoire, celle de son propre peuple, les Cris des Plaines du Nord.

Aujourd'hui, les toiles d'Allen Sapp, bien plus que celles de tout autre artiste canadien, sont axées sur la famille et la communauté. Même quand il n'y a aucun personnage sur un tableau, son titre ou son contenu fait allusion à la présence de personnes qui forment une partie intime de sa mémoire. Pendant des milliers d'années la communauté et la survie allèrent de pair pour le peuple d'Allen. Ses grands-parents firent partie de la dernière génération à pratiquer le nomadisme et la chasse et de la première à faire la transition vers les traités et la vie dans une réserve. Leur sens de la communauté avait été intensifié par un nouvel impératif : la survie face à l'anéantissement du bison, le développement vers l'ouest et les restrictions gouvernementales visant l'assimilation culturelle.

Allen Sapp était imprégné de la vision du monde que partageaient ses grands-parents et ceux de leur génération. Pour eux, la terre, la famille, la spiritualité et la communauté étaient toutes intimement liées et son art en témoigne. Dans la vision traditionnelle du monde qu'Allen connaissait quand il était enfant la générosité faisait partie intégrante du bonheur et, à n'en pas douter, de la survie. Un don ou un talent individuel était une "bénédiction spirituelle" qui devait être partagée avec la famille et avec la communauté élargie.

"L'artiste est considéré comme étant doué spirituellement pour le bien commun de la communauté."
– Bob Boyer

Cela peut aider à expliquer le fort sentiment d'appartenance à la communauté exprimé dans l'art de Sapp. Ce qui est encore plus important, c'est que cela explique aussi pourquoi de nombreux Cris s'identifient fortement aux tableaux d'Allen Sapp, revendiquant son histoire comme étant la leur – une histoire qui leur appartient tout comme elle appartient à leurs petits-

gift of art as having been encouraged and formed by the old ones in the interest of the community and future generations.

"[Allen's] teachers were excellent, honourable people the way they taught him ... You know when you see a picture of Allen's ... He puts a spirit in that drawing ... and that's the connection that the young people will get."
– Alma Kytwayhat

Allen, now in his mid-70s, continues to be very active in his culture, participating in regional and international gatherings. Some of what he paints has been inspired by the pow wows, feasts, or Sundances that he has attended in recent years. Other themes are inspired by events from his early childhood. Together these paintings bear witness to the enduring vitality of his people and culture. They also speak to the fulfillment of his grandparents' hope that the Nehiyawak ways would survive and not become victim to assimilation or indifference.

Indoor Pow Wow at Sweetgrass Reserve
– a pow wow Allen recalled from the 1930s

Pow-wow en salle à la réserve Sweetgrass
– un pow-wow dont Allen se souvenait des années 1930

In 1955 Allen married. His wife, Margaret, spent several years in the sanatorium in Prince Albert. It was there in 1957 that their son, David, was born.

In 1963, after the death of his grandparents, Allen, his wife and son moved to the small city of North Battleford and rented the humble upper story of a house. In this flat Allen set up his easel and began to paint.

"Allen and Margaret, they moved from one place to another, they were very poor. He'd do little sketch drawings, or paints. He continued practicing ... They came to stay here, North Battleford. They were very poor ... There wasn't anything I could do. They were hungry

enfants. Ils voient son don artistique comme ayant été encouragé et formé par les anciens dans l'intérêt de la communauté et des générations futures.

"Les maîtres [d'Allen] étaient excellents, des gens honorables dans leur manière d'enseigner. ... On le sait quand on voit une peinture d'Allen ... Il donne un esprit à ce dessin. ... et c'est ce rapport que nos jeunes vont saisir."
– Alma Kytwayhat

Allen, qui a maintenant plus de 75 ans, continue à être très actif au sein de sa culture et participe à des rassemblements régionaux et internationaux. Certains thèmes de ses peintures s'inspirent des pow-wows, des festins ou des danses du soleil auxquels il a assisté au cours des dernières années, d'autres thèmes s'inspirent d'événements de sa petite enfance. Ensemble, ces peintures attestent de la vitalité persistante de son peuple et de sa culture. Elles témoignent également des vœux de ses grands-parents qui se sont réalisés que les coutumes de Nehiyawak survivent et ne deviennent pas victimes de l'assimilation ou de l'indifférence.

Allen s'est marié en 1955. Sa femme, Margaret, a passé plusieurs années au sanatorium de Prince Albert. C'est là que leur fils David est né en 1957.

En 1963, après le décès de ses grands-parents, Allen, sa femme et leur fils ont déménagé dans la petite ville de North Battleford où ils ont loué l'humble premier étage d'une maison. C'est dans cet appartement qu'Allen installa son chevalet et commença à peindre.

"Allen et Margaret, ils déménageaient d'un endroit à l'autre, ils étaient très pauvres. Il faisait des petits croquis ou des peintures. Il continuait à s'exercer ... Ils sont venus habiter ici à North Battleford. Ils étaient très pauvres ... Je ne pouvais rien faire. Ils avaient faim parfois, si pauvres ...

at times, so poor ... I admonished him ... 'Think of manitow, *and our mother, and your guardian, the spirit guardian. You will get help.' So one day he told me of a doctor he had met."*
— Alex Sapp, Allen's father

Je l'ai averti ... 'Pense à manitow *et à notre mère, à ton gardien, l'esprit gardien. Tu vas recevoir de l'aide.' Alors un jour il m'a parlé d'un docteur qu'il avait rencontré."*
— Alex Sapp, le père d'Allen

One winter morning in 1966, Sapp ventured timidly into the North Battleford Medical Clinic trying to sell his paintings to the doctors. There he met the clinic's director, Doctor Allan Gonor. This meeting was to begin a relationship that would change both men's lives.

Allan Gonor immediately saw significance and

The Pow Wow
— a pow wow Allen recalled from the 1990s

Le pow-wow
— un pow-wow dont Allen se souvenait des années 1990

Un matin au cours de l'hiver 1966, Sapp se risqua timidement dans la clinique de North Battleford dans l'espoir d'y vendre ses peintures aux médecins. C'est là qu'il rencontra le directeur de la clinique, le docteur Allan Gonor. Cette rencontre allait être le début d'une relation qui allait changer la vie des deux hommes.

Allan Gonor vit tout de suite la portée et les possibilités du travail de Sapp. Lors de la deuxième visite

possibilities in Sapp's work. On Allen's second visit Doctor Gonor was immediately drawn to a painting of Chief Sam Swimmer. He bought it at once and gave Allen money for supplies.

"This is much better," I told him ... "You should paint what you know."

Doctor Gonor asked Allen if he would paint more of the people and places he remembered from the reserve. This invitation to paint from his life experience opened a door to Allen Sapp's heart. At first the paintings seemed to just pour out. Doctor Gonor had hoped to buy what Allen could produce but quickly realized that Allen was painting one or two paintings a night. In order to assist Allen, Doctor Gonor began to seek advice from professionals across Canada.

It was not without reservation that Sapp was painting the memories of his past. His life to that point had been the same as any other Aboriginal of his generation. He had contended with the harsh reality of residential school and the systematic efforts to suppress

d'Allen chez le docteur Gonor, ce dernier fut immédiatement attiré par une peinture du chef Sam Swimmer. Il l'acheta sur-le-champ et donna de l'argent à Allen pour s'acheter des fournitures artistiques.

"C'est beaucoup mieux," lui dis-je ... "Tu devrais peindre ce que tu connais."

Le docteur Gonor demanda à Allen s'il allait peindre davantage de personnes et d'endroits dont il se souvenait de la réserve. Cette invitation à peindre à partir de son expérience de vie ouvrit une porte dans le cœur d'Allen Sapp. Au début les peintures semblaient affluer. Le docteur Gonor avait espéré acheter ce qu'Allen pourrait produire mais il se rendit vite compte qu'Allen peignait une ou deux toiles par soir. Le docteur Gonor commença à consulter des professionnels à travers le Canada pour pouvoir aider Allen.

Ce n'était pas sans réserve que Sapp peignait les souvenirs de son passé. Sa vie jusque-là avait été la même que celle de n'importe quel autre Autochtone de sa génération. Il avait été aux prises avec la dure réalité du

his language and culture. He too had been subject to the restrictive pass and permit system that confined both his and his grandparents' generation to the reserve and effectively undermined their capacity to succeed as farmers. He was painfully aware of the gap between his people and his white sisters and brothers, and he could not imagine why anyone would be interested in paintings that depicted the humble simplicity of his former reserve life.

"At first Allen feared to show (in his paintings) a broken window, a damaged farm implement, anything that indicated want or poverty."
– Allan Gonor

It was through the encouragement of his own father and people like Wynona Mulcaster, an art professor at the University of Saskatchewan, that Allen's concerns were set aside. Doctor Gonor had arranged to drive Allen to see Wynona upon the advice of the director of the Winnipeg Art Gallery, Doctor Ferdinand Eckhardt.

In September of 1968, Wynona invited Allen to show his paintings on the grounds of her home in Saskatoon. The show was a great success, but this favourable response from a largely artistically cultured crowd in no way prepared them for the overwhelming public response to his first major exhibition only seven months later. It was Easter weekend at the Mendel Art Gallery in Saskatoon; a show of sixty-one oils and acrylics had been assembled and hung. When the doors finally opened that weekend some 13,000 viewers passed through the gallery. At the conclusion of the opening night most of the sixty-one paintings had been sold. That Easter weekend in 1969 began an explosion of interest in and fascination with Sapp's work that resulted in shows from London to Los Angeles. Reviews on his shows came from all

Allan Gonor, Wynona Mulcaster and Allen Sapp in 1968 at Allen's first exhibition

Allan Gonor, Wynona Mulcaster et Allen Sapp en 1968 à la première exposition d'Allen

pensionnat et les efforts systématiques pour supprimer sa langue et sa culture. Lui aussi avait été en butte au système de laissez-passer et de permis restrictifs qui avait confiné à la réserve sa génération et celle de ses grands-parents et qui avait vraiment sapé leur capacité de réussir en tant qu'agriculteurs. Il ne connaissait que trop le fossé qui séparait son peuple de ses sœurs et de ses frères blancs et il ne parvenait pas à imaginer pourquoi quiconque s'intéresserait à des peintures qui représentaient l'humble simplicité de son ancienne vie passée dans une réserve.

"Au début, Allen craignait de montrer (dans ses peintures) une fenêtre brisée, de la machinerie agricole endommagée, tout ce qui indiquait un manque ou la pauvreté."
– Allan Gonor

C'est grâce à l'encouragement de son propre père et de personnes comme Wynona Mulcaster, professeure d'art à l'Université de la Saskatchewan, que les inquiétudes d'Allen se dissipèrent. Sur les conseils du docteur Ferdinand Eckhardt, le directeur de la Galerie d'art de Winnipeg, le docteur Gonor avait convenu de conduire Allen chez Wynona.

En septembre 1968, Wynona invita Allen à exposer ses peintures dans le jardin de sa résidence à Saskatoon.

L'exposition remporta un grand succès mais cette réaction favorable venant d'une foule de gens pour la plupart très cultivés sur le plan artistique n'avait aucunement préparé Allen à la réponse extrêmement chaleureuse du public lors de sa première grande exposition qui eut lieu sept mois plus tard. C'était durant la fin de semaine de Pâques à la Galerie Mendel de Saskatoon ; l'exposition affichait une collection de soixante et une peintures, huiles et acryliques. Quand les portes s'ouvrirent enfin cette fin de semaine-là, quelques 13 000 observateurs franchirent le seuil de la galerie. À la fin de la soirée de vernissage la plupart des soixante et une toiles étaient vendues. Cette fin de semaine de Pâques 1969 fut le début d'une explosion d'intérêt et de fascination pour le travail de Sapp, qui eut comme résultat des expositions de Londres à Los Angeles. Les critiques sur ses expositions arrivaient de

quarters. He was applauded by the public as a 20th century painter it could relate to and by the critics as a painter whose style created

"*illusionism so arresting as to constitute a revelation.*"
– *Daily Telegraph of London, 1969*

By now Allen, himself, had begun to grasp the full implications of his success, but his reaction was modest and in character. He let his hair grow into long braids that he tied up with deerskin. He began to wear denim, cowboy boots, beaded medallions and a headband along with his cowboy hat. He was a descendant of the great Chief Poundmaker and had begun to understand the pride of being able to live that.

In May of 1976, Allen visited New York to attend the opening of his show at the Hammer Galleries. Diana Loercher of the Christian Science Monitor observed, of Sapp and his work:

He let his hair grow into long braids that he tied up with deerskin
Il se laissa pousser les cheveux et se fit de longues tresses qu'il attachait avec des liens en peau de chevreuil

"*He has great reverence for the land, a tradition in Indian Religion, and derives much of his inspiration from nature. A radiant light permeates most of his paintings. … It is evident that not only his art but his identity is deeply rooted in Indian culture.*"

It was this deeply-rooted identity that acted to stabilize Allen during these years of great attention and ensured his values and priorities remained true. As Doctor Gonor observed:

"*His values have not changed. Because of the traditional Indian belief in sharing … he cares more about looking after his relations and participating in religious ceremonies and dances than painting even though he cannot keep up with the demand.*"

toutes parts. Le public l'applaudit comme étant un peintre du 20ᵉ siècle auquel il pouvait s'identifier et les critiques d'art comme étant un peintre dont le style avait créé

"*un illusionnisme si saisissant qu'il constituait une révélation.*"
– *Daily Telegraph of London, 1969*

À cette époque-là, Allen avait aussi commencé à saisir toute la portée de son succès, cependant sa réaction était modeste, tout à fait dans son caractère. Il se laissa pousser les cheveux et se fit de longues tresses qu'il attachait avec des liens en peau de chevreuil. Il commença à porter du denim, des bottes de cow-boy, des médaillons perlés et un bandeau, le tout accompagné de son chapeau de cow-boy. C'était un descendant du grand chef Poundmaker et il avait commencé à comprendre la fierté de pouvoir vivre ça.

En 1976, Allen se rendit à New York pour assister au vernissage de l'une de ses expositions aux Hammer Galleries. Voici ce que Diana Loercher du Christian Science Monitor observa au sujet de Sapp et de son travail :

"*Il a une grande vénération pour la terre, une tradition dans la religion indienne, et une grande partie de son inspiration vient de la nature. Une lumière radieuse imprègne la plupart de ses peintures. … Il est évident que non seulement son art mais son identité sont profondément enracinés dans la culture indienne.*"

C'est cette identité bien ancrée qui a servi à stabiliser Allen durant ces années de grande attention à son égard et qui a assuré qu'il demeure fidèle à ses valeurs et à ses priorités. Selon les observations du docteur Gonor :

"*Ses valeurs n'ont pas changé. En raison de sa croyance au partage selon la tradition indienne. … Il a plus à cœur de s'occuper de sa famille et de participer à des cérémonies religieuses et à des danses que de peindre, même s'il ne peut pas répondre à la demande.*"

The significance of Sapp's roots and the stability and vision they offered him cannot be understated. The other important influence and stabilizing factor in his life was the friendship that grew between himself and Doctor Allan Gonor. Dr. Gonor was a Russian-born Jew whose own humble beginnings had left him with an openness to all creeds and cultures. Gonor was a kind and gentle man whose appreciation of art stemmed from his intense fascination with and appreciation of all world cultures. Gonor's gift was his insight and enthusiasm that spurred and motivated not only Allen Sapp but other emerging artists like author W. P. Kinsella, and Inuit artists David Ruben Piqtoukun and Abraham Anghik.

By 1974 Allen Sapp had found commercial success and attained widespread attention. He had been the subject of a book, *Portrait of the Plains*, by then Lieutenant-Governor of Alberta Grant MacEwan. His

He met a number of important people, including Prime Minister Pierre Elliott Trudeau
Il a rencontré plusieurs personnes importantes y compris le Premier ministre Pierre Elliott Trudeau

life and art were also the subject of a CBC and National Film Board documentary, and he had met a number of important people, including Prime Minister Pierre Elliott Trudeau. All of these events gave evidence of his popularity and the respect he had gained, but little did he know he was about to experience one of his greatest milestones as an artist.

In December 1975, Allen Sapp was elected to the Royal Canadian Academy of Arts (R.C.A.A.). Election to the R.C.A.A. means something far beyond commercial success for an artist. The historic role pursued by the R.C.A.A. through the years has been to maintain the highest standards in the cultivation of the fine and applied arts in Canada. Members of the R.C.A.A. represent a cross-section of Canada's most

L'importance des racines de Sapp et la stabilité et la vision qu'elles lui ont offertes ne peuvent être sous-estimées. L'autre influence importante et stabilisatrice dans sa vie fut l'amitié qui s'est développée entre le docteur Allan Gonor et lui. Le docteur Gonor était un juif né en Russie dont les humbles origines l'avaient laissé ouvert à toutes les croyances et les cultures. Gonor était un homme d'une grande gentillesse pour qui l'appréciation de l'art venait de sa fascination intense et de son appréciation de toutes les cultures du monde. Gonor offrit sa perspicacité et son enthousiasme qui ont encouragé et motivé non seulement Allen Sapp mais d'autres artistes en herbe tel l'écrivain W. P. Kinsella et les artistes inuits David Ruben Piqtoukun et Abraham Anghik.

Dès 1974, Allen Sapp avait réussi sur le plan commercial et sa renommée était faite. Il avait fait l'objet d'un livre *Portrait of the Plains* écrit par le lieutenant-gouverneur albertain de l'époque, Grant MacEwan. Sa vie et son art avaient également été le sujet d'un documentaire de l'Office national du film et de CBC. Il avait aussi rencontré plusieurs personnes importantes, y compris le Premier ministre Pierre Trudeau. Tous ces événements témoignaient de sa popularité et du respect qu'il avait acquis, mais il était loin de savoir qu'il était sur le point de vivre l'une des expériences les plus marquantes de sa vie d'artiste.

En décembre 1975, Allen Sapp fut élu à l'Académie royale des arts du Canada (l'ARC). Pour un artiste, être élu à l'ARC représente bien plus que le succès sur le plan commercial. Le rôle historique qu'a poursuivi l'ARC au fil des années a été de maintenir les plus hautes normes afin de cultiver les beaux-arts et les arts appliqués au Canada. Les membres de l'ARC représentent un éventail d'artistes

distinguished artists. Election to membership was the acknowledgement of the quality and value of Sapp's work by one of the most demanding and discriminating groups concerned with the arts in Canada, his own peers. As each new award or acknowledgement came, Allen's reaction remained modest and simple. In 1980 he met Princess Margaret and presented her with one of his paintings. In 1981 a book, *A Cree Life: The Art of Allen Sapp*, was released and found its way across Canada as a popular best-seller.

In 1985 he faced the news that his good friend and patron, Doctor Allan Gonor, had died while visiting in Thailand.

Allen, himself, had experienced the death of many members of his own family, including the death of his son, David, in 1977, and had struggled deeply with the loss of loved ones. It was his determination and strength of character that seemed to guide Allen through these difficult times. This strength of character was soon to be acknowledged as having significance and value to his community, and the community that was to call him their own began to expand far beyond the bounds of the Red Pheasant Reserve or the city of North Battleford.

On December 5, 1985, Allen Sapp became one of the first eight recipients of the Saskatchewan Order of Merit alongside Saskatchewan icons like Tommy Douglas. This award is given in recognition of individual excellence or contributions to the social and economic well-being of the province and its residents. It was one of the first indications that Allen was being recognized, not only as an artist, but as an individual and a citizen. He had become recognized as a force in

qui sont parmi les plus distingués du Canada. Être élu membre représente la reconnaissance qu'un des groupes les plus exigeants et avertis en matière d'art au Canada, ses propres pairs, accorde à la qualité et à la valeur du travail de Sapp. À chaque nouveau prix ou nouvelle reconnaissance, la réaction d'Allen demeurait modeste et simple. En 1980, il rencontra la Princesse Margaret et lui présenta un de ses tableaux. En 1981 parut un livre, *A Cree Life: The Art of Allen Sapp*, qui devint un best-seller populaire à travers le Canada.

C'est en 1985 qu'il apprit la mauvaise nouvelle que son grand ami et mécène, le docteur Allan Gonor, était décédé au cours d'un voyage en Thaïlande.

Allen avait perdu de nombreux membres de sa propre famille, y compris son fils David en 1977 et il en avait vivement souffert. C'est sa détermination et sa force de caractère qui semblèrent le guider lors de cette période difficile. Cette force de caractère allait bientôt être reconnue comme ayant une signification et une valeur pour sa communauté, et la communauté qui l'avait adopté comme l'un des siens commença à dépasser les limites de la réserve Red Pheasant ou de la ville de North Battleford.

Le 5 décembre 1985, Allen Sapp fut l'un des huit premiers récipiendaires du Saskatchewan Order of Merit aux côtés de grands personnages de la Saskatchewan comme Tommy Douglas. Ce prix est accordé en guise de reconnaissance pour l'excellence individuelle ou pour des contributions au mieux-être social et économique de la province et de ses résidents. Ce fut l'une des premières indications que l'on reconnaissait Allen non seulement en tant qu'artiste mais en tant que personne et citoyen. On commençait à le reconnaître désormais comme une force dans la renaissance de la culture des

On December 5, 1985, Allen Sapp became one of the first eight recipients of the Saskatchewan Order of Merit. Allen Sapp with Tommy Douglas (far left) and other recipients of the Saskatchewan Order of Merit

Le 5 décembre 1985, Allen Sapp fut l'un des huit premiers récipiendaires du Saskatchewan Order of Merit. Allen Sapp avec Tommy Douglas (à l'extrême gauche) et les autres récipiendaires du Saskatchewan Order of Merit

the renaissance of the First Nations culture, and his art and life story were seen as a beacon for other aspiring native artists. His art was also beginning to create a bridge for other cultures to come to understand the Indian way of life and the world view underlying it.

It came as no surprise that in 1986, at the "New Beginnings" Native Art Show in Toronto, Allen Sapp was singled out as one of the Senior Native Artists in Canada, *"whose contributions to the present renaissance of native art and culture will only be measured by history."*

That simple observation seemed almost prophetic in light of what was about to occur. In January 1987 the Governor General of Canada, Jeanne Sauvé, appointed Allen Sapp an Officer to the Order of Canada, which is a means of recognizing outstanding achievements and honouring those who have given service to Canada, to their fellow citizens or to humanity at large. That award marked the beginning of a series of honours that have now come to include the opening, in 1989 in North Battleford, of the Allen Sapp Gallery: The Gonor Collection (the only public gallery bearing the name of a living artist), the Saskatchewan Arts Board Lifetime Achievement Award (1997), an honourary doctorate from the University of Regina (1998), a National Aboriginal Lifetime Achievement Award (1999) and the Governor General's Award for Illustration of a Children's Book (2003).

The creation of the 2005 national touring exhibition *Through the Eyes of the Cree and Beyond* is an important and significant milestone

Allen Sapp receiving the Order of Canada from Governor General Jeanne Sauvé

Allen Sapp recevant l'Ordre du mérite du Canada de l'ancienne Gouverneure générale Jeanne Sauvé

Premières nations; son art et l'histoire de sa vie étaient considérés comme un phare pour d'autres artistes autochtones en herbe. Son art commençait également à créer un pont pour que d'autres cultures en viennent à comprendre le style de vie des Indiens et la vision du monde qui lui est sous-jacente.

Ce ne fut donc pas étonnant qu'en 1986, à l'exposition d'art autochtone "New Beginnings" à Toronto, Allen Sapp fut choisi comme l'un des principaux artistes autochtones au Canada : *"dont seule l'histoire pourra mesurer les contributions à la renaissance actuelle de l'art et de la culture autochtones."*

Cette simple observation semble presque prophétique à la lumière de ce qui était sur le point de se produire. En janvier 1987 la Gouverneure générale du Canada, Jeanne Sauvé, nomma Allen Sapp Officier de l'Ordre du Canada, un titre qui reconnaît des réalisations exceptionnelles et qui honore ceux et celles qui ont rendu service au Canada, à leurs concitoyens ou à toute l'humanité. Cette décoration marqua le début d'une série d'honneurs qui comprennent désormais l'ouverture en 1989 à North Battleford de la galerie Allen Sapp : la collection Gonor (la seule galerie publique à porter le nom d'un artiste vivant), le Prix d'excellence pour l'ensemble de son œuvre par le Saskatchewan Arts Board (en 1997), un doctorat honorifique de l'Université de Regina (en 1998), un prix national autochtone d'excellence pour l'ensemble de son œuvre (en 1999) et la Médaille du Gouverneur général pour les illustrations d'un livre pour enfants (en 2003).

La création de l'exposition itinérante nationale de 2005 *À travers le regard des Cris et au-delà* est un jalon important et significatif pour Allen Sapp. Son exposition

for Allen Sapp. His 1995 national touring exhibition "Kiskayetum" was an excellent retrospective organized by the MacKenzie Art Gallery in Regina and curated by his close friend, the late Bob Boyer.

The 2005 exhibition is not a career retrospective, rather it is an exhibition that examines the full significance of Sapp's art to his own people. Its genesis was the 2002 creation of a site for the Virtual Museum of Canada. This award-winning site used digital technology to capture the thoughts and stories of the Elders of Allen's generation as they reflected upon the memories invoked by his paintings. Their insights, digitally combined with Allen's paintings, weave the larger story of a history yet untold. This unique version of their own history, told not by academics, historians, or pundits, but by ordinary people, has become the basis of the touring exhibition. Inspired by Allen's paintings, the Elders' stories speak of the joys and sorrows of a people that struggled against great odds and significant obstacles to give their children a better future founded upon a rich and proud past.

As his father foresaw, Allen's art and story have come to reveal the story of his people, illuminating it for all to see.

After more than half a century, the prophetic dream of Nootokao, who had placed her hand upon his forehead as Allen lay sick, had now come to pass – "*There was a purpose for this frail one who made such a determined effort to live.*"

– Dean G. Bauche, Director/Curator
Allen Sapp Gallery

"Then one night I had a dream ... This must have been what I dreamed about, where he stands today."
– Alex Sapp

"Puis une nuit j'ai fait un rêve ... c'est à ça que j'ai dû rêver, où il se trouve aujourd'hui."
– Alex Sapp

itinérante nationale de 1995 "Kiskayetum" organisée par la Mackenzie Gallery de Regina et préparée par son ami intime, le regretté Bob Boyer, fut une excellente rétrospective.

L'exposition de 2005 n'est pas une rétrospective de sa carrière mais plutôt une exposition qui examine toute la signification de l'art de Sapp pour son propre peuple. La genèse de sa carrière a été à l'origine de la création en 2002 d'un site pour le Musée virtuel du Canada. Ce site primé se sert de la technologie numérique pour capter les pensées et les histoires des Aînés de la génération d'Allen alors qu'ils retracent les souvenirs évoqués par ses peintures. Leurs réflexions, combinées numériquement aux peintures d'Allen, tissent une plus grande toile d'une histoire qui n'a jamais été racontée. Cette version unique de leur propre histoire, racontée non par des universitaires, des historiens ou des pontes mais par des gens ordinaires, est devenue la base de cette exposition itinérante. Inspirés par les peintures d'Allen, les histoires des Aînés parlent des joies et des peines d'un peuple qui a lutté contre des forces supérieures et de grands obstacles pour donner à ses enfants un avenir meilleur fondé sur un passé riche et fier.

Tout comme son père l'avait présagé, l'art d'Allen et son histoire ont fini par révéler l'histoire de son peuple en l'illuminant pour que tous la voient.

Après plus d'un demi-siècle, le songe prophétique de Nootokao, qui avait posé sa main sur le front d'Allen lorsqu'il gisait malade, se réalisait. "*Il y avait une raison d'être pour ce frêle adolescent qui avait lutté de façon si déterminée pour rester en vie.*"

– Dean G. Bauche, directeur/conservateur
Galerie Allen Sapp

THE ART OF ALLEN SAPP

"It is safe to say ... that if it had not been for Maggie Soonias there would not have been Allen Sapp 'the artist'."

– Two Spirits Soar

"On peut affirmer sans trop s'avancer ... que s'il n'y avait pas eu Maggie Soonias il n'y aurait pas eu Allen Sapp, 'l'artiste'."

– Two Spirits Soar

"I was sitting by the table thinking what to draw, nobody around, me and my grandmother alone in that place. She comes to my mind, the one who raised me. I speak to her a little bit, ask her if it's okay to sketch her face. I never done that before.

"She says – 'Yes, Grandson, that will be fine, while I am still here.' My grandmother was thinking about that too. 'You can draw my face. It is not too far off for me to hear no more.' She tells me that, sitting very quiet. When I finished I told her it was done. That was only a quick job. Later I done a good job."

– Allen Sapp

"J'étais assis près de la table en train de réfléchir à ce que j'allais dessiner, il n'y avait personne d'autre que ma grand-mère et moi, seuls dans cet endroit. Je pense à elle, c'est elle qui m'a élevée. Je lui parle un peu, je lui demande si je peux dessiner son visage. Je ne l'ai jamais dessiné avant.

Elle dit – 'Oui, mon petit-fils, c'est bien tant que je suis encore ici.' Ma grand-mère pensait à ça aussi. 'Tu peux dessiner mon visage. Dans peu de temps je n'entendrai plus.' Elle me dit ça, assise tranquille. Quand j'ai fini, je lui ai dit que le portrait était terminé. J'avais fait ça vite. Plus tard j'en ai fait un mieux."

– Allen Sapp

Drawing My Grandmother
Dessinant ma grand-mère
ê-tâpasinahwak nôhkom

1972   acrylic on canvas   Allen Sapp

"If you lose money you can get it again. If you lose people they don't come back any more."
– *Allen Sapp*

"Si vous perdez de l'argent vous pouvez encore en avoir. Si vous perdez des gens, ils ne reviennent plus."
– *Allen Sapp*

"One of the things about families during that era is the grandmother was usually the one constant influence for young people.

"Grandparents tended to be very kind and gentle and resourceful, knowledgeable. They were people you could count on. And they encouraged you, they helped you, they guided you, they taught you, they were not so concerned with day-to-day survival in a sense. It was more that they could transcend the necessities of survival and begin to think again about other things that were important … your emotional well being, or your intellectual development. So, in a sense they were the teachers, they were more than caregivers."

    – Wes Fineday

"Une des choses concernant les familles à cette époque-là c'est que la grand-mère était généralement une influence constante pour les jeunes.

Les grands-parents étaient très gentils et doux, débrouillards et avertis. C'étaient des gens sur qui vous pouviez compter. Et ils vous encourageaient, ils vous aidaient, ils vous guidaient, ils vous enseignaient des choses, Ils ne se préoccupaient pas tant que ça de la survie quotidienne d'une certaine manière. C'était plutôt qu'ils pouvaient transcender les nécessités de la survie et commencer à repenser à d'autres choses qui étaient importantes … votre bien-être émotionnel ou votre développement intellectuel. Alors d'une certaine manière ils étaient vos maîtres, ils étaient plus que des aidants."

    – Wes Fineday

At My Grandmother's Grave

Sur la tombe de ma grand-mère

nôhkom oyîkwahaskânihk

1971   acrylic on canvas   Allen Sapp

"If someone died there was always a pipe ceremony. Actually, any important event in your life was often preceded by a pipe ceremony. The pipe, for us, was important in that it represented spirituality. With a pipe ceremony you call upon the spirit helpers of the Creator. You ask the Creator to witness what is happening here and, with the prayer, ask that we be blessed. … It was not everyone who had a pipe. … That was something that had to be earned. But once it was earned it was honoured and respected in the community. So whenever there was an important event like a funeral or a wake or a feast … it was always preceded by a pipe ceremony."

– Wes Fineday

"Si quelqu'un mourait il y avait toujours une cérémonie du calumet. En fait, avant chaque événement important de votre vie il y avait une cérémonie du calumet. Et le calumet était important pour nous parce qu'il représentait la spiritualité. Avec la cérémonie du calumet, vous appelez les esprits guérisseurs du Créateur. Vous demandez au Créateur d'être témoin de ce qui se passe ici-bas, et avec la prière que nous soyons bénis … Ce n'était pas tout le monde qui avait un calumet … C'était quelque chose qu'il fallait mériter. Mais une fois qu'on l'avait mérité, il était honoré et respecté dans la communauté. Alors quand il y avait un événement important comme un enterrement, une veillée funèbre ou un festin … Il y avait toujours une cérémonie du calumet avant."

– Wes Fineday

There was always a pipe ceremony for any important event in your life.

Il y avait toujours une cérémonie du calumet pour tout événement important dans votre vie.

Someone Died Here

Quelqu'un est mort ici

awiyak ôta kî-pôni-pimâtisiw

1970   acrylic on canvas   Allen Sapp

The story that Allen Sapp tells began long before his birth.

L'histoire que raconte Allen Sapp a commencé bien avant sa naissance.

"A man could hunt, might get one moose … or whatever, and you would take what you could home. Often it was up to the woman and her relations to go and get what had been left behind. And so they would do the skinning and the cutting up and the bringing home. … They would have women and young girls learning how to cut meat into real thin strips so they could be hung over a frame or a post with a fire to dry them, to smoke them. These tools, the fleshing tools and the scraping tools, these were women's tools. Often they would be handed down through the generations. You would get your grandmother's scraper … if you had earned the right and had proven that you were capable of using it."

— Wes Fineday

"Un homme pouvait chasser, pouvait attraper un orignal … ou autre chose, et vous rameniez ce que vous pouviez à la maison. Souvent c'était à la femme ou à des membres de sa famille d'aller chercher ce qui avait été laissé derrière. Et ils s'occupaient de dépecer, de découper la viande et de la ramener à la maison. … Il y avait des femmes et des jeunes filles qui apprenaient à découper la viande en lanières très minces pour pouvoir les suspendre sur un cadre ou un poteau avec un feu pour les sécher, pour les fumer. Ces outils, les décharnoirs et les racloirs, c'était des outils de femmes. Souvent on se les passait d'une génération à l'autre. On vous donnait le racloir de votre grand-mère … si vous aviez mérité ce droit et que vous aviez prouvé que vous étiez capable de vous en servir."

— Wes Fineday

Maggie Soonias' Elk Horn Hide Scraper　　　　**Racloir à cuir en bois de wapiti de Maggie Soonias**

My Grandfather's Campsite
Le Campement de mon grand-père
ita kâ-kî-kapêsit nimosôm

1967   acrylic on canvas   Allen Sapp

Scraping a Hide
Raclage d'une peau
ê-mihkicikêt

2004   acrylic on canvas   Allen Sapp

Great Grandfather's Buffalo Hunt
La chasse aux bisons de l'arrière grand-père
nicâpân ê-nôcihât paskwâwi-mostoswa

1967   acrylic on canvas   Allen Sapp

Because Allen was raised by his grandparents his work reveals an intimate understanding of the "old ways", community and Cree world view.

Parce qu'Allen a été élevé par ses grands-parents son travail rappelle une compréhension intime de "la vie d'antan", de la communauté et de la vision du monde des Cris.

"Someone has passed on, and you have a feast. … That was important: to honour your ancestors. And often you would see people sitting in a circle and there would be places (spaces) that would seem like … someone had been sitting there and had left or the circle might not seem complete. And yet it was always said that we should always leave places so that the spirits of our ancestors or the spirit helpers of Creator would come and join in the circle with us. It was not that the circle was empty or the circle was broken, it was because of our human frailties. We are not able to see the spirits but it does not mean they are not there."

– *Wes Fineday*

"Quelqu'un mourait, et vous organisiez un festin. … C'était important d'honorer vos ancêtres. Et souvent on voyait des gens assis en cercle et il y avait des endroits (des places vides) et il semblait que quelqu'un avait eu l'habitude de s'asseoir là et qu'il était parti ou que le cercle ne paraissait pas complet. Et pourtant on disait qu'il fallait toujours laisser de la place pour que les esprits de nos ancêtres ou les esprits guérisseurs du Créateur puissent venir se joindre à nous autour du cercle. Ce n'était pas que le cercle était vide ou brisé, c'était à cause de notre fragilité humaine. Nous ne pouvons pas voir les esprits mais ça ne veut pas dire qu'ils ne sont pas présents."

– *Wes Fineday*

Fineday's Teapot Poundmaker First Nation

Similar to the teapot depicted in the painting "Feast at Little Pine Cemetery".

La théière de Fineday de la Première nation Poundmaker

Semblable à la théière représentée dans le tableau "Festin au cimetière de Little Pine".

Feast at Little Pine Cemetery

Festin au cimetière de Little Pine

ê-wîhkohkêhk yîkwahaskânihk wâskitôwiyinînâhk

1984   acrylic on canvas   Allen Sapp

"In this painting you see there are three old men over there on the left (page 33), sitting. There are usually four that would be there that would have their pipes. … You have the four old men, and you have the singers, and then you have the people who have made vows. Vows they made when they were asking for blessings, for help, for healing in times of sickness. … Attendants you could say; they could be considered as having come to support these people who have made vows. Support them and help them to find the strength to carry their vows through. And then the whistles that they blew, made out of eagle wing, wing bones, or leg bones … Human ears find it hard, and sometimes impossible, to even hear, never mind understand the language of spirit. … It sounds like whistling to us, and, for those of us who don't understand whistling, whistling is whistling."

– *Wes Fineday*

"Dans un tableau comme celui-ci vous voyez qu'il y a trois hommes âgés assis là-bas à gauche (page 33). Généralement, il y en a quatre là avec leurs calumets … Vous avez les quatre hommes âgés, vous avez les chanteurs et puis les gens qui ont fait des vœux. Les vœux qu'ils ont faits quand ils demandaient des bénédictions, de l'aide, la guérison quand ils étaient malades. … On pourrait dire des accompagnateurs; ils pouvaient être considérés comme une sorte de soutien pour ces gens qui avaient fait des vœux. Les soutenir et les aider à trouver la force de réaliser leurs vœux. Et puis les sifflets dans lesquels ils sifflaient, faits avec une aile d'aigle, les os des ailes ou les os des pattes … Les oreilles humaines trouvent ça dur et quelquefois c'est impossible de les entendre même, encore moins de comprendre le langage de l'esprit. … Pour nous ça ressemble à des sifflements. Et pour ceux d'entre nous qui ne comprennent pas les sifflements, les sifflements sont des sifflements."

– *Wes Fineday*

Blowing the Prayer Whistles

Soufflant dans les sifflets de prière

Sundance at Red Pheasant

Danse du soleil à Red Pheasant

ê-nipâkwêsimohk mikisiwacîhk

1974   acrylic on canvas   Allen Sapp

"Generosity has always been a traditional value in our culture; it is interpreted as a gesture of love and respect. As an example, during the Sundance Ceremony, people give offerings to the spirits and to each other in order to receive future spiritual guidance. Before a ceremony ends, a feast is given for the people and for the spirits of the departed."

– *Pat Deiter McArthur.*

"La générosité a toujours été une valeur traditionnelle dans notre culture; on l'interprète comme un geste d'amour et de respect. Par exemple, pendant la cérémonie de la danse du soleil, les gens donnent des offrandes aux esprits et s'en donnent les uns les autres pour recevoir de futurs conseils spirituels. Avant la fin d'une cérémonie, on offre un festin aux gens et aux esprits des disparus."

– *Pat Deiter McArthur.*

"Once that drum has been used (has been awakened) … there are traditional ways to store it. Usually you would make a bag for it and you would keep it with sweetgrass and tobacco, because when you are going to use it you have to smudge it, and, in the smudging, too, it is not out of order to offer it a bit of tobacco and to ask that the tobacco offering be considered same as a pipe for a pipe ceremony."

– Wes Fineday

"Une fois que le tambour a été utilisé (qu'on l'a réveillé) … il y a des manières traditionnelles de l'entreposer. Généralement vous avez un grand sac pour ça et vous le gardez avec du foin d'odeur et du tabac. Parce que, quand vous allez vous en servir, vous devez le purifier, et lors de la purification il est de mise d'offrir un peu de tabac et de demander que l'offrande de tabac soit considérée comme un calumet pour une cérémonie du calumet."

– Wes Fineday

Hand Drum

– Allen Sapp Gallery Collection

Tambour

– Collection de la galerie Allen Sapp

Playing the Drums

Jouant du tambour

mistikwaskihkwa ê-matwêhwâcik

1970   acrylic on canvas   Allen Sapp

The Drum

"Two primary types of drums exist among the Cree. The small hand drum is covered with hide on one side and used as an accompaniment in many ceremonies and gambling games. The double-headed drum is constructed by molding a flat birch board into a rim and stretching a hide over it. The drumhead is heated prior to use to produce a better tone."

– *Pat Deiter McArthur*

Le tambour

"Chez les Cris il existe deux principaux types de tambours : Le petit tambour recouvert de peau d'un côté et qui est utilisé pour accompagner de nombreuses cérémonies et des jeux d'argent, et le tambour sur cadre qui est fabriqué en moulant une bande plate de bouleau dans un cadre et en tendant de la peau par-dessus. La peau de tambour est chauffée avant de s'en servir pour produire un meilleur son."

– *Pat Deiter McArthur*

"In the old days too there were gatherings much in the same way that there were feasts … like celebrations that were more community oriented … pow wow, *pwâtisimowin* (the Sioux dance) it is called in Cree, but that took more than a family to sponsor. … It would be the society of dancers that would sponsor and organize that part of a cultural celebration, but it would involve entire communities. It would be open … to people: anyone who was interested in coming. It was … like old gatherings when people would come together to celebrate, to trade medicines, to do many different kinds of trading. You know, there was a whole social aspect to it. … So it was an opportunity for different camps and even different tribes to come together without any kind of threat, to just come and relax and enjoy life and, if you were a dancer, to dance."

– *Wes Fineday*

"Dans l'ancien temps il y avait des rassemblements de la même manière qu'il y avait des festins … comme des fêtes qui étaient davantage pour la communauté … pow-wow, *pwâtisimowin* (la danse Sioux) comme on l'appelle en cri, mais il fallait plus d'une famille pour parrainer … C'était l'association de danseurs qui parrainait et qui organisait cette partie de la fête culturelle, mais des communautés entières participaient. C'était ouvert … aux gens: à toute personne intéressée à venir. C'était … comme les rassemblements dans le temps, quand les gens se retrouvaient pour fêter, pour troquer des plantes médicinales et pour faire toutes sortes de trocs. Vous savez, il y avait tout un aspect social à ça. … Alors c'était une occasion pour différents camps et même différentes tribus de se regrouper sans aucune sorte de menace, de venir simplement, se reposer et apprécier la vie, et si vous étiez danseur, de danser."

– *Wes Fineday*

Pow Wow at The Battlefords

Pow-wow aux Battlefords

ê-pwâtisimohk nôtinitowi-sîpîhk

1971　acrylic on canvas　Allen Sapp

"Pow wow … people coming together, old ways again. It is good to go back to old ways so young people can learn, so they won't get lost, kids learning from their folks. It's nice for mothers, fathers to speak to children, to rest and visit and laugh, to be happy together."

– Allen Sapp

"Un pow-wow … des gens qui se rassemblent, encore les coutumes d'autrefois. C'est bon de revenir aux coutumes d'autrefois pour que les jeunes puissent apprendre, pour qu'ils ne soient pas perdus, les enfants qui apprennent des leurs. C'est bien pour les mères, les pères de parler à leurs enfants, de se reposer, de rendre visite aux autres, de rire et d'être heureux ensemble."

– Allen Sapp

His grandparents were part of the last generation to live the nomadic hunting way of life and of the first to sign treaties and make the transition to reserve and agriculture.

Ses grands-parents firent partie de la dernière génération à pratiquer le nomadisme et la chasse et de la première à signer les traités et à faire la transition vers la réserve et l'agriculture.

Union Jack

Elder Joe Stick from Onion Lake described the significance of the Union Jack this way:

"We should have a lot of respect for the Union Jack. …That is the flag that was signed with our sacred stem, our pipe, [for] as long as the sun shines, grass grows, and rivers flow, that was what was promised us … They wrote the 'X' [signing the treaties] on behalf of the pipe, the pipe was there to look after them, the pipe was sacred to the Queen when she signed, her representatives signed the treaty. Let's respect the other side. Let's respect the treaty. … Let's respect each other."

Le Union Jack

L'Aîné Joe Stick d'Onion Lake a décrit la signification du Union Jack de cette manière:

"Nous devrions avoir beaucoup de respect pour le Union Jack. …C'est le drapeau qui a été signé avec notre calumet sacré, tant que le soleil brillera, que l'herbe poussera, que les rivières couleront, c'est ce qu'on nous a promis … Ils ont mis le 'X' [pour signer les traités] au nom du calumet, le calumet était là pour s'occuper d'eux, le calumet était sacré pour la Reine quand elle a signé, quand ses représentants ont signé le traité. Respectons l'autre côté. Respectons le traité …Respectons-nous les uns les autres."

Treaties

"… And since these treaties were considered to be on that same level as a vow witnessed by the Creator and spirit powers, people would make a point to try and live up to them. Often that same recognition of the agreement was not understood by … the government … not understanding the spiritual significance to the same degree that our Elders in our communities understood them."

– *Wes Fineday*

Les traités

"… Et comme les traités étaient considérés être au même niveau qu'un vœu devant le Créateur et les pouvoirs des esprits, les gens se faisaient un devoir d'essayer de s'y conformer. Souvent cette même reconnaissance de l'entente n'était pas comprise par … le gouvernement … qui ne comprenait pas la signification spirituelle au même degré que nos Aînés dans nos communautés."

– *Wes Fineday*

Inside Dance Hall at Stoney Reserve

À l'intérieur de la salle de danse à la réserve Stoney

pîhcâyihk nîmihitowikamikohk pwâsîmônâhk

1970   acrylic on canvas   Allen Sapp

Chief Sam Swimmer

Le chef Sam Swimmer

okimâhkân Sam Swimmer

1966   oil on canvas panel Allen Sapp

This painting depicts Chief Sam Swimmer in the treaty uniform issued as a part of the treaty process.

Ce tableau représente le chef Sam Swimmer dans son uniforme de traité qui avait été donné comme faisant partie du processus de traité.

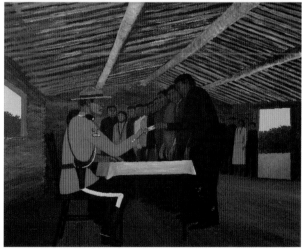

Receiving Treaty Money

Recevant l'argent du traité

ê-tipahamâtohk

1993   acrylic on canvas   Allen Sapp

Gone to Eat

Parti manger

aspin ê-nitawi-mîcisot

1972   oil on canvas   Allen Sapp

"I used to go with grandpa to get a permit to sell willow pickets. You got to tell how many hundred, like if you have two hundred willow pickets you got to have a permit for two hundred. If you have a load of wood, you have to have a permit. Without that you can't take it out of the reserve, cause they'll pinch you."

— *Solomon Stone*

"J'allais avec mon grand-père chercher le permis pour vendre des piquets en saule. Il fallait leur dire combien de centaines, par exemple si vous aviez deux cents piquets il fallait un permis pour deux cents piquets. Si vous aviez une charge de bois, il fallait avoir un permis. Sans ça vous ne pouviez pas la sortir de la réserve, parce qu'ils vous pinçaient."

— *Solomon Stone*

The Fence Needs Fixing

La clôture a besoin d'être réparée

ohcitaw ta-kî-nânapâcihtâhk mênikan

1968   acrylic on canvas   Allen Sapp

Fences

Fences symbolized the "new way" brought about by the treaties and the encroaching European culture. The traditional view of the land was that it was sacred, belonging to no one, it was there for everyone. The "new way" meant land was parceled, sold and fenced.

Les clôtures

Les clôtures symbolisaient la "nouvelle vie" amenée par les traités et la culture européenne envahissante. La vision traditionnelle de la terre était qu'elle était sacrée, qu'elle n'appartenait à personne, qu'elle était là pour tout le monde. La "nouvelle vie" signifiait que la terre était divisée en parcelles, vendue et clôturée.

Watching Them Fix the House

Regardant les hommes réparer la maison

ê-kanawâpamakik ê-nânapâcihtâcik wâskahikan

1986   acrylic on canvas   Allen Sapp

"But those log houses sure weren't warm. …
There was no foundation … and then they start
building from there and if you didn't bank it, it
would be very cold from the floor. … You had to
have two stoves – one cook stove and one heater."

   – *Irene Fineday*

"I'd stomp my feet in that mud, helping out
that way. They'd plaster the walls, take out the old
ones [plaster] and put them back in the hot water
to make it soft. They did that every fall. If they did
a good job, they wouldn't have to do it for two
years time."

   – *Jonas Semaganis*

"Mais ces cabanes en rondins n'étaient vraiment pas
chaudes … Il n'y avait pas de fondation … et puis quand
ils commencent à les construire de là et si vous ne faisiez
pas de talus, c'était très froid du sol … Il fallait deux
réchauds, un pour la cuisine et l'autre pour le chauffage."

   – *Irene Fineday*

"Je tapais fort avec mes pieds dans cette boue en aidant
de cette manière. Ils plâtraient les murs, enlevaient les
anciens [plâtrages] et les mettaient dans l'eau chaude pour
les ramollir. Les Cris, ils faisaient ça tous les automnes.
S'ils faisaient un bon travail, ils n'avaient pas à le refaire
avant deux ans."

   – *Jonas Semaganis*

Looking for a Log

À la recherche d'un rondin

ê-na-nitonawât mistikwa

1975   acrylic on canvas   Allen Sapp

Building a Cabin

Construction d'une cabane

ê-wâskahikanihkêt mistikwa ohci

1981   acrylic on canvas   Allen Sapp

In spite of the outward changes in lifestyle it was clear that their values,
their world view, remained the same.

En dépit des changements apparents dans les modes de vie, il était clair que leurs valeurs,
leur vision du monde étaient restées les mêmes.

Four People on a Sleigh

Quatre personnes sur un traîneau

ê-nêwicik papêhkikahwânihk

1972   acrylic on canvas   Allen Sapp

Stopping to Talk

On s'arrête pour parler

ê-nakîcik aciyaw ta-kiyokâtocik

1974   acrylic on canvas   Allen Sapp

Previous page: Four People on a Sleigh

"On holidays or Christmas people drove over to some friends to get food and drink together. Some singing songs and playing a drum in the house. Sometimes the kids stayed home, looked after by the grandmother, often the kids went with them.

"When I was a little boy, my brothers and Stella and me, I remember we pulled a blanket over us in the sleigh, my father driving the team. Only my mother was away, she was in the San. That was Christmas Day a long time ago."

– *Allen Sapp*

Page précédente: Quatre personnes sur un traîneau

"Pendant les vacances ou à Noël les gens allaient en traîneau voir des amis pour manger et boire ensemble. Certains chantaient des chansons et jouaient du tambour dans la maison. Quelquefois les enfants restaient à la maison, ils s'occupaient de la grand-mère. Souvent, les enfants allaient avec eux.

Quand j'étais petit garçon, mes frères, Stella et moi, je me rappelle qu'on tirait une couverture sur nous dans le traîneau, mon père menait l'attelage. Seule ma mère était absente, elle était au sanatorium. C'était un jour de Noël il y a longtemps."

– *Allen Sapp*

Making a Rope for the Horse
Fabriquant une corde pour le cheval
ê-apihkâtahkik pîminahkwân
mistatimwa ohci

1976   acrylic on canvas   Allen Sapp

Slower Pace

"People used to have time for each other. They would stop and talk and visit. Today people don't have time for each other any more."

– Jonas Semaganis

Un rythme plus lent

"Les gens passaient du temps ensemble. Ils s'arrêtaient, parlaient, se rendaient visite. Aujourd'hui, les gens n'ont plus le temps de passer du temps les uns avec les autres."

– Jonas Semaganis

Untitled miniature #8
Miniature sans titre N° 8
câpasinahikanis 8 êkâ
kâ-wîhcikâtêk

1970   acrylic on canvas   Allen Sapp

Old-Fashioned Hand Game

Jeu de mains à l'ancienne

kayâsi-pakêsêwin

1973   acrylic on canvas   Allen Sapp

Bones used in Traditional Hand Game
  – Allen Sapp Gallery collection

Osselets utilisés pour le jeu de mains traditionnel
  – Collection de la galerie Allen Sapp

Playing 1-2-3

Jouant à 1-2-3

pêyak-nîso-nisto ê-mêtawêcik

1975   acrylic on canvas   Allen Sapp

In spite of the fact that Allen's mother died young, the memory of women and their influential role is a central theme in Allen's work.

En dépit du fait que la mère d'Allen est morte jeune, la mémoire des femmes et de leur rôle influent est un thème central dans le travail d'Allen.

Baby was Crying

Bébé pleurait

ê-kî-mâtot awa oskawâsis

1971　acrylic on canvas　Allen Sapp

Baby was Crying

"The mother is looking after the baby. They wrapped the baby in moss to keep it dry in the old days. The baby was tied in the swing so it couldn't fall out. They used to put me in one of those things when I was little. In those days babies didn't use diapers. This was the way when I was born on the reserve. The baby got food from its own mother then. He was too young to get it from the cow."

– Allen Sapp

Bébé pleurait

"La mère s'occupe du bébé. On enveloppait le bébé dans de la mousse pour le garder au chaud dans l'ancien temps. Le bébé était attaché dans la balançoire pour ne pas tomber. Dans le temps, on me mettait dans une de ces choses-là quand j'étais petit. En ce temps-là les bébés n'avaient pas besoin de couches. C'était comme ça quand je suis né dans la réserve. Le bébé était nourri par sa propre mère. Il était trop jeune pour être nourri par la vache."

– Allen Sapp

Allen's mother, Agnes, holding her son, Allen, in the moss bag made in 1924.

Agnes, la mère d'Allen, tenant son fils dans le sac de mousse fait en 1924.

Allen Sapp's Moss Bag

This moss bag was used in 1928 for Allen, the oldest son in the Sapp family. It was made by Allen's Aunt Jemima in 1924, when she was sixteen. Jemima died the following year. Over the years it has been used with all of Allen's brothers and sisters. Today it belongs to Simon Sapp (Allen's brother) and his wife, Theresa. It was used for each of their four children and for their grandchildren.

Le sac de mousse d'Allen Sapp

Ce sac de mousse a été utilisé en 1928 pour Allen, le fils aîné de la famille Sapp. Il avait été confectionné en 1924 par Jemima, la tante d'Allen, quand elle avait seize ans. Jemima mourut l'année suivante.

Au fil des années, il a été utilisé par tous les frères et toutes les sœurs d'Allen. Aujourd'hui il appartient à Simon (le frère d'Allen) et à sa femme Theresa. Il a servi à chacun de leurs quatre enfants et à leurs petits-enfants.

Baby is Sleeping

Bébé dort

ê-nipât awa oskawâsis

1970   acrylic on canvas   Allen Sapp

It is said that the moss bag and cradleboard provided the child with a sense of the security of the womb, while at the same time teaching them patience and encouraging physical strength. Elders tell stories of children who, as infants had been secured in cradleboards, took to walking almost immediately upon being provided the opportunity.

On dit qu'un sac de mousse et une planche porte-bébé donnaient à l'enfant un sentiment de sécurité comme s'il était dans le ventre de sa mère, tandis qu'en même temps ça lui apprenait la patience et ça encourageait la force physique. Les Aînés racontent des histoires d'enfants qui avaient été mis dans des planches porte-bébé et qui s'étaient mis à marcher aussitôt après en avoir eu l'occasion.

Beaded Cradleboard

Muscowpetung First Nation 1921

— *Royal Saskatchewan Museum collection*

Planche porte-bébé perlée

Première nation Muscowpetung en 1921

— *Collection du royal Saskatchewan Museum*

Cradleboard by Marcia Chickeness, created in 2002

— *Saskatchewan Arts Board Collection*

Planche porte-bébé créée en 2002

par Marcia Chickeness

— *Collection du Saskatchewan Arts Board*

The work of Marcia Chickeness, like that of Allen Sapp, is influenced and shaped by historic beliefs and traditions. At the same time their work reveals the face of a contemporary culture that is alive and well.

Le travail de Marcia Chickeness, comme celui d'Allen Sapp, est influencé et façonné par les croyances et les traditions historiques. Ils révèlent en même temps le visage d'une culture contemporaine qui est bien vivante.

Lady Doing Beadwork

Dame en train de coudre des perles

ê-mîkisistahikêt awa iskwêw

1971   acrylic on canvas   Allen Sapp

Inside My Old Home a Long Time Ago

Dans ma vieille maison il y a longtemps

pîhcâyihk nîkihk kayâs

1970   acrylic on canvas   Allen Sapp

"At the Soonias place … that's where my mother and father found each other. I stayed with my grandfather and grandmother Soonias. They wanted me there, like a son, their son. I wanted to be living with my grandparents. My father didn't want me to do that at first but my mother was sick and away at the San many times. That was my old place on Red Pheasant Reserve."

– Allen Sapp

"Chez les Soonias … c'est là que ma mère et mon père se sont rencontrés. Je suis resté avec mon grand-père et ma grand-mère Soonias. Ils voulaient que je sois là comme un fils, leur fils. Je voulais vivre avec mes grands-parents. Mon père ne voulait pas mais au début ma mère était malade et elle a dû aller plusieurs fois au sanatorium. C'était mon ancien chez moi à la réserve Red Pheasant."

– Allen Sapp

Baking Bannock

Cuisson du bannock

ê-pahkwêsikanihkêt

1969   acrylic on canvas   Allen Sapp

Picking Roots

Cueillette de racines

ê-mônahaskwêcik

1973   acrylic on canvas   Allen Sapp

Digging Stick
 – *made by*
 Clarence Swimmer

Bâton fouisseur
 – *fabriqué par*
 Clarence Swimmer

"Mostly … [women knew] medicines. A lot of that knowledge … about the uses and approaching it and picking it and preparation, processing … and generally it was older women.

These women would take out the little boys and girls who they would teach to identify medicines. … And these older women would supervise and show people how to clean them, the parts that you needed, if the plants had to be separated. They would be talking to you and telling you stories about medicines."

– *Wes Fineday*

"C'était surtout les femmes qui connaissaient les plantes médicinales. Une grande partie de ces connaissances… sur les usages et comment les approcher, les cueillir, les préparer et les traiter … les femmes plus âgées faisaient ça généralement.

Ces femmes amenaient les petits garçons et les petites filles et leur apprenaient à identifier les plantes médicinales. Ces femmes plus âgées surveillaient et montraient aux gens comment les nettoyer, les parties dont vous aviez besoin, si les plantes devaient être séparées. Elles vous parlaient et vous racontaient des histoires sur les plantes médicinales."

– *Wes Fineday*

We Shared all Foods

"When I was a young boy we ate roots; roots were eaten. Wild carrots dug from the ground. We ate medicine herbs, things to be boiled like wild rhubarb, berries, cherries, currants. We walk along going many miles for wild rhubarb to put in soup. Young people today don't know about that. We dug wild turnips, wild onions, and we did it all by walking. We shared all foods around to the people on the reservation, sharing, in the old days, sharing. For all sickness there is herbs, roots. He, manitow, makes it so people can't wipe out all herbs. This son of mine, Allen, I teach him these things."

– Alex Sapp (Allen's father)

Nous partagions tous les aliments

"Quand j'étais petit garçon, nous mangions des racines, ça se mangeait les racines. Des carottes sauvages que l'on déterrait. Nous mangions des herbes médicinales, des choses qu'on faisait bouillir comme la rhubarbe sauvage, les baies, les cerises et les groseilles. Nous faisions des kilomètres à pied pour trouver de la rhubarbe sauvage pour en mettre dans la soupe. Les jeunes aujourd'hui ne savent pas ça. Nous déterrions des navets sauvages, des oignons sauvages et on faisait tout ça en marchant. Nous partagions toutes les nourritures avec les gens de la réserve, partager, dans l'ancien temps, partager. Pour toutes les maladies il y avait des herbes, des racines. manitow, lui, fait en sorte que les gens ne puissent pas détruire toutes les herbes. Mon fils Allen, je lui apprends toutes ces choses."

– Alex Sapp (le père d'Allen)

Cooking Potatoes

Cuisson des pommes de terre

ê-kîsisahk askipwâwa

1969   acrylic on canvas   Allen Sapp

Waiting for Water to Boil

En attendant que l'eau bouille

ê-pêhot nipiy ta-ohtêyik

1975   acrylic on canvas   Allen Sapp

Maggie's Copper Pot

This copper pot belonged to Allen's grandmother, Maggie Soonias. Copper pots like this were highly valued utensils used frequently to make *maskihkîwâpoy* (tea, liquid medicine).

La marmite en cuivre de Maggie

Cette marmite en cuivre a appartenu à Maggie Soonias, la grand-mère d'Allen. Les marmites en cuivre comme celle-ci étaient des ustensiles précieux utilisés fréquemment pour faire du *maskihkîwâpoy* (thé, plantes médicinales sous forme de liquide).

Making a Crazy Blanket

Confection d'une courtepointe

ê-nanâtohkokwâsot

1974   acrylic on canvas   Allen Sapp

**As a boy … you spent a lot of time with your male relatives.
These men were your teachers and mentors.**

**Si vous étiez un garçon … vous passiez beaucoup de temps avec les hommes
de votre famille. Ces hommes étaient vos maîtres et vos mentors.**

Mentors and Teachers

"As a boy, after you were past the age of six, you spent a lot of your time with your male relatives. They instilled the importance of community. That's where you learned your work ethic, how to hunt, set snares, ride horses and farm. These men were your teachers and mentors. They took you to ceremonies and taught you songs and how to play the drum. As you grew older, you would do that for your nephews."

– *Wes Fineday*

Mentors et maîtres

"Si vous étiez un garçon, après l'âge de six ans, vous passiez beaucoup de temps avec les hommes de votre famille. Ils vous faisaient comprendre l'importance de la communauté. C'est là qu'on apprenait le fondement moral du travail, comment chasser, comment tendre des collets, comment monter à cheval et cultiver la terre. Ces hommes étaient vos maîtres et vos mentors. Ils vous amenaient aux cérémonies, vous apprenaient des chansons et comment jouer du tambour. En vieillissant, vous faisiez la même chose pour vos neveux."

– *Wes Fineday*

Men Visiting

Hommes en visite

nâpêwak ê-kiyokêcik

1989   acrylic on canvas   Allen Sapp

They Came to Visit His Brother

Ils sont venus rendre visite à son frère

ê-kî-pê-kiyokawâcik ostêsa

1975   acrylic on canvas   Allen Sapp

"When Allen's grandpa died, Allen lived with his grandma, in the old log shack. The old lady sold all the cattle. But Allen kept the horses and chickens. Allen didn't have no income, he use to take wood to Cando, which is our home town, 12 miles from the reserve. He use to sell wood for $5.00 a load. Many times, 40 below zero, he had hardships."

– Leonard Nicotine

"Quand le grand-père d'Allen est mort, Allen est allé vivre avec sa grand-mère dans la vieille cabane en rondins. La vieille dame a vendu tout le bétail. Mais Allen a gardé les chevaux et les poulets. Allen n'avait pas de revenu, il amenait du bois à Cando, notre ville natale, à douze miles de la réserve. Il vendait le bois 5 $ le chargement. Très souvent, il faisait 40 degrés au-dessous de zéro et il avait de la misère."

– Leonard Nicotine

Blowing Snow

Poudrerie

ê-pîwahk

1972   acrylic on canvas   Allen Sapp

The Cowboy

"I remember a cold winter day one time …
Alex Nicotine borrowed the horse from his friend
to go out there and find his own horses that had
wandered away. In my picture he found them.
Alex will chase them back to his own home."

– *Allen Sapp*

Le cow-boy

"Je me rappelle d'une froide journée d'hiver une fois
… Alex Nicotine avait emprunté le cheval d'un ami pour
aller chercher ses propres chevaux qui s'étaient éloignés.
Dans mon tableau, il les a trouvés. Alex les poursuivait
pour les ramener chez lui."

– *Allen Sapp*

The Cowboy

Le cow-boy

mostosowiyiniw

1968   acrylic on canvas   Allen Sapp

"You would also be taught about things that were considered important. Not only to think about yourself, but to think of others, to be considerate, to be kind. To be compassionate, to remember that you are not alone. That you are a part of something larger, you are part of a family. That family is part of a community, that community is part of a greater environment. And even the environment, the earth, is part of creation."

—*Wes Fineday*

"On vous enseignait aussi des choses qui étaient considérées comme importantes … Non seulement de penser à vous, mais de penser aux autres, d'être prévenant, d'être gentil, de faire preuve de compassion, de se souvenir que vous n'êtes pas tout seul, que vous faites partie de quelque chose de plus grand. Vous faites partie d'une famille. Cette famille fait partie de la communauté et cette communauté fait partie d'un environnement plus grand. Et même l'environnement, la terre, fait partie de la création."

—*Wes Fineday*

Late for the Meeting

En retard pour la réunion

wî-mwêstasisinwak kâ-mâmawapihk

1972   acrylic on canvas   Allen Sapp

"He recalls his father shooting a rabbit, skinning it in the bush in winter, then saying, 'Now we can eat. I've brought along some bannock, some tea – we'll make a fire and have lunch.'"

    – *W.P. Kinsella,* Two Spirits Soar

"Il se rappelle de son père tirant sur un lapin, le dépeçant dans le bois en hiver, puis disant, 'Maintenant nous pouvons manger. J'ai apporté du bannock, du thé – nous allons faire un feu et déjeuner.'"

    – *W.P. Kinsella,* Two Spirits Soar

Warming Up

On se réchauffe

ê-awasocik

1975   acrylic on canvas   Allen Sapp

"It was not surprising to see families travelling about, either, going to do something and doing it together. Like going to cut hay for instance. You would have the men who were going out to do the actual cutting and raking and stacking, but you'd also have the women coming along and setting up camp and doing the cooking. It was your home. The haying fields, the haying lands, were your home for the time that you were doing it. You would live in a tent there and the kids would be along … You were part of the community and you needed to fulfill that role in the community."

– *Wes Fineday*

"Ce n'était pas surprenant de voir des familles voyager soit pour aller chercher quelque chose ou pour faire quelque chose ensemble. Pour aller couper du foin par exemple. Il y avait les hommes qui allaient couper le foin, le ratisser et l'empiler, mais il y avait aussi les femmes qui venaient, qui installaient un campement et qui faisaient la cuisine, c'était votre maison. Ces terres à foin étaient votre foyer le temps que vous faisiez ça. Vous viviez dans une tente et le enfants vous accompagnaient … Vous faisiez partie de la communauté et vous deviez remplir ce rôle dans la communauté."

– *Wes Fineday*

Washtubs, like so many other things, had multiple uses. They were even reused as camp stoves.
 * This washtub is similar to the washtub depicted in the painting "Moving to a Different Place".

Les bacs à laver le linge, comme beaucoup d'autres choses, avaient des utilisations multiples. On les utilisait souvent comme réchauds.
 Ce bac à laver le linge est semblable au bac à linge représenté dans le tableau "Départ vers un autre endroit".

Moving to a Different Place

Départ vers un autre endroit

ê-âhcipicicik

1968   acrylic on canvas   Allen Sapp

Broken Wheel on Reserve

Roue brisée à la réserve

kâ-pîkopayik tihtipipayîs iskonikanihk

1977   acrylic on canvas   Allen Sapp

Sapp's art depicts his people's successful transition to the "new way" (agriculture).

**L'art de Sapp représente la transition réussie de son peuple
vers cette "nouvelle vie" (l'agriculture).**

Doing a Grease Job

Faisant un graissage

ê-tômâpiskinikêt

1992   acrylic on canvas   Allen Sapp

Raking Hay

Râtelage du foin

ê-mâwasakwaskosîwêt

1970   acrylic on canvas   Allen Sapp

"Lots of work to do in summer. First the mowing. We sharpened up the mower knife on a big turnstone, John or me splashing water from an old tobacco tin. Two horses were hitched up, one of the men would do the driving, I drove the team when I was older, kids running behind. Little mice had nests there, as we mowed along we saw them running out all ways. Ducks' nests were hid there too; fox holes and hills the gophers made. Soon it was time for the raking if the weather was dry. We used to give the rake from one family to the other, sharing that rake. It lifted a load when we pulled a handle, then dropped the load where we wanted."

– *Allen Sapp*

"Il y avait beaucoup de travail à faire l'été. D'abord tondre. Nous aiguisions la lame de la tondeuse sur une grosse meule. John ou moi on aspergeait de l'eau d'une vieille boîte de tabac. On attelait deux chevaux, un des hommes les menaient. J'ai mené l'attelage quand j'étais plus grand, les enfants couraient derrière. Des petites souris avaient leurs nids là et, quand on tondait, on les voyait partir dans tous les sens. Il y avait aussi des nids de canards cachés; des terriers de renards et des monticules que les gauphres avaient faits. Bientôt le moment était venu de ratisser s'il faisait sec. Nous avions l'habitude de nous passer le râteau d'une famille à l'autre, on se partageait le râteau. Ça montait une charge quand nous appuyions sur le manche, puis ça faisait tomber la charge où on voulait."

– *Allen Sapp*

Loading Hay

Chargement du foin

ê-pîhtaskosîwêcik

1970   acrylic on canvas   Allen Sapp

"[In this painting] It seems like there is something wrong with this horse's face, but actually … in the summer time when you're working out in the field there were always flies and mosquitoes … bothering the horses, so they … had devised the canvas [that would be cut into strips like fringes] as a protection you might say."

– *Wes Fineday*

"[Dans ce tableau] On dirait que quelque chose ne va pas avec la tête du cheval. Mais en fait l'été quand on travaillait dans les champs il y avait toujours des mouches et des moustiques qui embêtaient le cheval, alors on avait fait une toile (découpée en lanières comme des franges) pour le protéger dirons-nous."

– *Wes Fineday*

A Pass and Permit System

Allen's paintings reveal that, in spite of obstacles, many of his people made a successful transition to the "new way" (agriculture). Unfortunately, by the late 1880s, just as they were demonstrating a capacity for success, white farmers in Manitoba and the North-West Territories (present day Saskatchewan and Alberta) complained that Indian farmers were "unfair" competition because of the government assistance offered in making their transition to farming. In response to the complaints the government enacted the "Peasant Farm Policy" in 1889 which resulted in dismantling of the "tribal" or "communist systems" in favour of small farms of only a few acres.

This policy was implemented in spite of the "Pass and Permit" system which already restricted the First Nations from leaving the reserve or selling their produce on or off the reserve. The Permit system required for selling produce was instituted in 1881. This law, although not actively enforced in later years (1950s onward), was not officially revoked until 1995. The Pass system was instituted in 1885 in an attempt to put an end to the Sundance. (It was repealed in 1951.)

Many First Nations' farmers, like Allen's grandfather, Albert Soonias, proved to be very successful and hard working. (He had over 100 head of cattle.) The travel and trade restrictions imposed upon people like Allen's grandfather meant that they were property rich and cash poor. First Nations' communities and individuals never benefited from the right of the open and free trade afforded the other farmers of his generation. Indeed, Indian farmers were not allowed to kill one of their own cows for consumption without a permit from the Indian agent.

Un système de laissez-passer et de permis

Les tableaux d'Allen révèlent qu'en dépit des obstacles une grande partie de son peuple a bien réussi à faire la transition vers cette "nouvelle vie" (l'agriculture). Malheureusement, vers la fin des années 1880, alors qu'ils faisaient preuve d'une capacité de réussir, les agriculteurs blancs du Manitoba et des Territoires du Nord-Ouest (la Saskatchewan et l'Alberta de nos jours) se sont plaints que les agriculteurs indiens constituaient une concurrence "injuste", (à cause de l'assistance gouvernementale qui leur avait été offerte pour effectuer cette transition vers l'agriculture). En réponse à ces plaintes, le gouvernement promulgua en 1889 "une politique agricole des paysans" qui eut comme résultat le démantèlement des "systèmes communistes ou tribaux" en faveur des petites fermes de quelques acres seulement.

Cette politique a été mise en place en dépit du système de "laissez-passer et de permis" déjà en place qui empêchait les Premières nations de quitter la réserve ou de vendre leurs produits dans la réserve ou à l'extérieur de la réserve. Le système de permis requis pour vendre des produits a été institué en 1881. Cette loi, bien qu'elle ne fût pas appliquée activement lors des dernières années (après les années 1950), n'a été révoquée officiellement qu'en 1995. Le système de laissez-passer a été introduit en 1885 pour essayer de mettre fin à la danse du soleil. (Il a été abrogé en 1951.)

De nombreux agriculteurs des Premières nations comme Albert Soonias, le grand-père d'Allen, se sont avérés très prospères et très travailleurs. (Il possédait plus de cent têtes de bétail.) Les restrictions de déplacement et de commerce imposées aux personnes comme le grand-père d'Allen signifiaient qu'ils étaient riches en biens mais pauvres en argent. Les communautés des Premières nations et les Indiens n'ont jamais tiré profit du droit au commerce ouvert et au libre-échange accordé aux autres agriculteurs de sa génération. À vrai dire, les agriculteurs indiens n'avaient pas le droit de tuer une de leurs propres vaches pour leur consommation personnelle sans obtenir de permis de l'agent des sauvages.

Men Threshing

Des hommes au battage

nâpêwak ê-pawahikêcik

1970   acrylic on canvas   Allen Sapp

"But at the time, being a child, I thought it was fun. You know, getting ready in the middle of the night, my brothers harnessing the horses and getting the hay … I thought it was exciting at the time, not knowing we were not allowed to sell hay without a permit."

– *Alma Kytwayhat*

"Mais en ce temps-là être un enfant, je pensais que c'était amusant. Vous savez, se préparer au milieu de la nuit, mes frères qui attelaient les chevaux et qui emmenaient le foin … je pensais que c'était passionnant à cette époque sans savoir que nous ne pouvions pas vendre le foin sans avoir de permis."

– *Alma Kytwayhat*

A Good Harvest

Une bonne récolte

takahki-manisikêwin

1994   acrylic on canvas   Allen Sapp

Two Brothers Going Home with a Load

Deux frères rentrant à la maison avec un chargement

nîso wîcisânak ê-kîwêhtatâcik maskosiya

1990   acrylic on canvas   Allen Sapp

Taking Water Home

Apportant de l'eau à la maison

ê-kîwêhtatât nipiy

1975   acrylic on canvas   Allen Sapp

"The horse was part of our life. They were obedient horses, never mistreated or anything like that … my dad said these horses were respected. According to my grandfather, these horses were put on earth for one specific purpose, that is to serve the people."

– *Jonas Semaganis*

« Le cheval faisait partie de notre vie. Les chevaux étaient obéissants, jamais maltraités ou des choses comme ça … Mon père disait que ces chevaux étaient respectés. D'après mon grand-père ces chevaux avaient été mis sur terre pour un but particulier, celui de servir les gens. »

– *Jonas Semaganis*

Going to Feed His Horses

Allant donner à manger à ses chevaux

ê-nitawi-asamastimwêt

1975   acrylic on canvas   Allen Sapp

My Grandfather's Ranch a Long Time Ago

Le ranch de mon grand-père il y a longtemps

itê kâ-kî-kanawêyimostoswêt kayâs nimosôm

1972   acrylic on canvas   Allen Sapp

"My grandfather had two, three stables for the cattle, big stables. Cattle was kept inside at night when winter nights was very cold. It was a big job putting up enough hay for the winter. I helped with that."

– *Allen Sapp*

"Mon grand-père avait deux, trois étables pour le bétail, de grandes étables. Le bétail restait dedans la nuit quand il faisait très froid l'hiver. C'était un gros travail de mettre assez de foin pour l'hiver. J'aidais à faire ça."

– *Allen Sapp*

Getting the Cows a Drink

Donnant à boire aux vaches

ê-nitawi-minahât mostoswa

1968   acrylic on canvas   Allen Sapp

"If you had a cow you could starve to death because you didn't have the right, according to the law, to butcher to provide for your own basic needs. All of these things were governed and determined by Indian agents who were the representatives of the government."

— *Wes Fineday*

"Si vous aviez une vache, vous pouviez mourir de faim parce que vous n'aviez pas le droit, d'après la loi, de la tuer pour vos propres besoins de base. Toutes ces choses étaient gouvernées et déterminées par les agents des sauvages qui étaient les représentants du gouvernement."

— *Wes Fineday*

Untitled miniature #4
Miniature sans titre N° 4
câpasinahikanis 4 êkâ
kâ-wîhcikâtêk

1970   acrylic on canvas   Allen Sapp

Untitled miniature #5
Miniature sans titre N°5
câpasinahikanis 5 êkâ
kâ-wîhcikâtêk

1970   acrylic on canvas   Allen Sapp

Man in Barn

Un homme dans une grange

nâpêw misatimowikamikohk ê-ayât

1972   acrylic on canvas   Allen Sapp

John Bear's Horses

Les chevaux de John Bear

John Bear otêma

1971   acrylic on canvas   Allen Sapp

Winter Horseshoe
 – *On loan from
    Kenneth Tootoosis*

Fer à cheval pour l'hiver
 – *prêt de
    Kenneth Tootoosis*

"Horses always played a very important role in the community. Even before reserves, and before farming and before that whole change in lifestyle. ... You know, people thought very highly of their horses. In fact, they often treated the horses either just as well or better than they treated themselves and their families. ... But you needed to take good care of your horses because often they were the determining factor in your ability to do things for yourself. ... There was not a lot that you could do without your horses."

– *Wes Fineday*

"Les chevaux ont toujours joué un rôle très important dans la communauté. Même avant les réserves, avant l'agriculture et avant ce style de vie complètement différent. ... Vous savez les gens avaient une très grande estime pour les chevaux. En fait, ils traitaient les chevaux aussi bien sinon mieux qu'ils se traitaient eux-mêmes et qu'ils traitaient leurs familles ... Mais il fallait bien prendre soin de vos chevaux parce qu'ils étaient souvent un facteur déterminant dans votre capacité de faire des choses pour vous. ... Il y avait beaucoup de choses que vous ne pouviez pas faire sans vos chevaux."

– *Wes Fineday*

"Hunting used to be a very spiritual experience. … The reason you need it is to stay alive, to be healthy. … Ceremony was a part of hunting. … The Creator knows how many animals there are on this land and, at the end of the day, when the Creator comes to check on the spirits, comes to check up on this earth, He will see we have taken one moose and He will see this tobacco we've offered to the spirit of this moose, and it was done with ceremony and respect in a sacred manner, and so the Creator will bless us by replacing this one that was taken. … The taking of life was not a game; it was serious business."

— *Wes Fineday*

"La chasse était une expérience très spirituelle. … La raison pour laquelle vous en avez besoin c'est pour rester en vie, pour être en bonne santé. … La cérémonie faisait partie de la chasse. … Le Créateur sait combien d'animaux il y a sur cette terre et, à la fin de la journée, le Créateur vient vérifier les esprits, vient vérifier la terre. Il verra si nous avons tué un orignal et il verra le tabac que nous avons offert à l'esprit de l'orignal et que cela a été fait avec cérémonie et respect d'une manière sacrée et alors le Créateur nous bénira en remplaçant celui qui a été tué. … ôter la vie n'était pas un jeu, c'était sérieux."

— *Wes Fineday*

Saddle
Cree-style designs with beadwork – beaded patches.
Traditional saddle used by Plains Cree.
Date unknown
– *From the collection of the Royal Saskatchewan Museum*

Selle
Motifs perlés de style cri – appliqués perlés.
Selle traditionnelle utilisée par les Cris des Plaines
Date inconnue
– *de la collection du Royal Saskatchewan Museum*

Chasing a Coyote

À la poursuite d'un coyote

ê-nawaswâtât mêstacâkanisa

1969   acrylic on canvas   Allen Sapp

Through the Eyes of the Cree

— L. Whiteman and L. Carrier

"It's good to know things like that are not forgotten."
— Irene Fineday

The paintings of Allen Sapp tell many stories. These paintings are a veritable journey into the memory of their creator. The Plains Cree traditional way of life resonates as though from the skin of a beautiful handmade drum. Allen Sapp, Kiskayetum (*kiskêyihtam*, He perceives it) shares warmly and freely of the gifts he was given; to portray his childhood experiences growing up in the 1930s and '40s on the harsh Saskatchewan Prairies. Stories spring from canvas. Memories dance in pure colour. Kiskayetum's life has been an array of experiences that he has painted with a palette that is full, not just with colours but with his own emotions. These emotions saturate each canvas with the joy, sorrow, gratitude, responsibility, love, respect and deep humility that define not only him but the values he has been entrusted to convey to future generations. He honours his role and responsibility as he carries on the oral tradition of his people. His gift as a storyteller utilizes images, not words, that remind the Elders of the importance of identity and cultural values. These values are intended for Sapp, as a grandson, and for his grandchildren and for theirs and so on. He explains, "I can't write a story or tell one in the white man's language so I tell what I want to say with my painting."

nêhiyaw kâ-isi-wâpahtahk

— L. Whiteman, L. Carrier (Jean Okimâsis êkwa *Arok Wolvengrey* ê-kî-itwêstamâkêcik ôma)

"mêtoni ê-kiskisihk kayâs kîkwaya. miywâsin êkâya ê-wanikiskisihk."
— Irene Fineday

otâpasinahikêwina awa *Allen Sapp* mihcêt âcimowina êkota astêyiwa. tâpwê piko mâna tâpiskôc okiskisiwinihk ê-is-îtohtêhk kâ-wâpahtamihk otâpasinahikêwina. mitoni mîna tâpiskôc êkota pêhtâkwaniyiw kayâs paskwâw-iyiniwak kâ-kî-pê-isi-pimâcihocik. *Allen Sapp, Kiskayetum* (kiskêyihtam) namôya sasâkisiw nayêstaw nôhtê-âsônamawêw otayisiyinîma anima kâ-kî-miyikowisit ê-tâpasinahahk anihi kâ-kiskisitotahk kâ-kî-pê-isi-ohpikit, *1930s* mîna *1940s* ê-akimiht awa askiy, ê-awasisiwit ê-kî-âyimaniyik ôta paskwâhk. mêtoni êkota âcimowina sôskwâc ohtakotêyiwa. kâ-kiskisihk anihi pakaski-wâpahcikâtêw ê-itasinâstêki. tâpwê awa kiskêyihtam nanâtohk kî-pê-isi-itâcihow êwako anima kâ-tâpasinahahk ê-miywâsiniyiki mîna tâpwê omôsihtâwin êkota ê-nôkwaniyik. êwakon ôhi omôsihtâwin êkota kâ-wâpahtamihk miyawâtamowin, pîkiskâtamowin, nanâskomowin, nâkatêyihtamowin, sâkihitowin, manâcimiwêwin, êkwa tapahtêyimisowin êwakon ôhi kâ-kî-miyikowisit ta-âsônamawât osk-âya ôtê pêci-nikân. kistêyihtam ôma kâ-isi-miyikowisit tâpitawi ê-âcimot. ê-tâpasinahahk anihi kâ-kiskisitotahk namôya katâc pîkiskwêw kita-âcimot êwakon ôki kêhtê-ayak kâ-kiskisomikocik iyikohk ê-kistêyihtâkwaniyiki ispîhtêyihtâkosiwina êkwa onêhiyâwiwiniwâw. wiya ôhi ohci wiya awa *Sapp*, ôsisimimâw, êkwa wîsta ôsisima, mîna otâniskotâpâna, mîna wîstawâw otâniskotâpâniwâwa. omisi itwêw, "namôya nikaskihtân ta-masinahamân âcimowin môy mîna ahpô nika-kî-âkayâsîmon ta-âcimoyân êkosi nitâcimowina nitâpasinahikanihk astêwa."

Everybody Dancing
pikw âwiyak ê-nîmihitocik

Indeed, the Creator has given Allen Sapp a special gift to paint pictures, but what is truly wondrous is his capacity to imbue these pictures in such a way as to stir the memories of the Elders. When the Elders look at these paintings they see and remember their past. As they are drawn back, with some sentimental nostalgia, the Elders begin to reconnect memory with the time and space where they grew up. In the process of recollection begins an important connection that fuses our present to the past and to the ancient generations of long ago.

The importance of Allen Sapp's work cannot be appreciated by seeing it simply as a collection of beautiful paintings. Equally important to note is the effect that these pictures have on the old people, particularly the Cree Elders. Look at these paintings through the eyes of their creator and you will learn of the world through the eyes of the Cree. Lessons about living in the harsh climate abound as the Elders look at Sapp's paintings and remember. Remembering is paramount to learning, especially when the lessons have been all but forgotten in our collective memories because of the circumstances of colonization. Remembering is resistance. When our Elders are stirred at these pictures of the recent past, they help young people learn about the shooting of rabbits; making dry meat (*kahkêwakwa*); how to make fish baskets; the way the stick has to be grooved out so the rope won't slide; how to find Seneca root (*mînisîhkês*) and other medicines and how and when to use them; to understand the importance of ceremonies, the prayers and the songs; the trees that were best for the tipi poles; the connection to the land; the connection to animals and to all living things.

At My Grandmother's Grave
nôhkom oyîkwahaskânihk

tâpwê awa *Allen Sapp* ê-kî-miyikowisit ta-nihtâ-tâpasinahikêt, mâka ayiwâk koskwêyihtâkwan iyikohk ê-isi-kaskihtât ta-tâpastât kayâs pimâcihowin êkwa ê-kiskisôhikoyit kêhtê-aya. ispîhk mâna kêhtê-ayak kâ-kitâpahtahkik ôhi tâpasinahikêwina kiskisiwak tânisi kâ-kî-pê-isi-pimâcihocik pêci nâway. êkwa ê-ati-kiskisicik, apisîs pîkiskâcihikowak, êkwa mâci-mâmitonêyihtamwak ita kâ-kî-tas-ôhpikicik. êwako ôma kiskisiwin kikiskisôhikonânaw tânitê ê-ohtaskanêsiyahk mîna kihci-kayâs iyiniwak.

êkâ ta-kî-itêyihtamihk awa *Allen Sapp* otâpasinahikêwina têpiyâhk piko ê-miyonâkwaniyiki mâka ta-kî-kistêyihtamihk iyikohk kâ-miywêyihtamihikocik mâna ôki nêhiyaw-kêhtê-ayak kâ-kanawâpahtahkik. kanawâpahtamok ôhi tâpasinahikêwina tâpiskôc awa otâpasinahikêw kâ-isi-wâpahtahk wiya êkota kika-kiskêyihtên tânisi nêhiyaw ê-isi-kiskêyihtahk ôma askiy. mêtoni êkota tâpasinahikêwinihk kêhtê-ayak wâpahtamwak kâ-kî-pê-isi-kiskinohamâhcik tânisi ta-isi-pimâcihocik ôta ôma askiy ayis ê-kî-nayêhtâkwahk. mêtoni piko ta-kiskisihk ka-kiskinwahamâkosihk, wâwîs pikw âwiyak êkwa ê-wanikiskisit ispîhk ohci môniyâwak kâ-takosihkik êkwa kâ-mâci-kistikêhk. nânakâsîwin anima kâ-kiskisihk. ispîhk mâna kikêhtê-âyiminawak kâ-kitâpahtahkik anihi tâpasinahikêwina kiskisôhikowak êkosi mâna kakwê-wîcihêwak osk-âya ê-kiskinohamawâcik tânisi ta-isi-nôtâposwêyit, ta-kâhkêwakohkêyit, tânisi ta-isi-watapîwatihkêyit, tânisi katâc anima miscikos ta-pasihkotamihk pîminahkwân êkâ ta-sôskopayik, tânisi ta-isi-nitawaskihkîwêyit, mînisîhkês mîna kotaka maskihkiya mîna tânisi ta-isi-âpacihtâyit, mîna tânispîhk kita-âpacihtâyit êkoni, ta-nisitohtamiyit ê-kistêyihtâkwaniyiki nêhiyaw-isîhcikêwina, kâkîsimowina êkwa nikamowina, tâniki aniki nawac mistikwak ta-âpacihimiht macêkinwa ohci, ta-manâcihtâyit askiy, pisiskiwa mîna, kahkiyaw kâ-pimâtisiyit mîna.

The lessons that emerge when the Elders look at the paintings are undeniably important. The paintings, combined with the Elders' stories, represent a framework of important traditional Cree teachings that have survived through the generations. In this survival story beats the heart of the Ancestors and within it flickers the hopeful flame of a culture that is alive.

These paintings take us back to a place and time when the Plains Cree had a simpler way of life. There was hardship, to be sure, but as you look back you can experience the beauty of a culture that has withstood the changes of the seasons and the changes of the times. Allen Sapp has found a way to portray the way of life of the Cree people, without oversimplifying or romanticizing.

This story is told through a child's eyes. These are the memories of a grandson whose heartfelt desire is to tell the story with honesty and humility. You feel the child's sense of vulnerability as he so accurately captures and depicts the details of his daily life, so much so that an undercurrent of longing for that moment builds within us.

Recapturing this past allows us, as First Nations People, to feel the pride in what was an honourable, beautiful way of life. The Elders speak of the moments captured in his paintings with fond recollection; he has been able to gently take them by the heart back to the moments of their childhood. Despite much bitterness and sadness, there is joy in the richness of the values of the Plains Cree culture.

Starting to Make a Tipi
Sapp's paintings represent a framework of important traditional Cree teachings.

ê-mâci-mânokêhk
nêhiyaw kihci-isîhcikêwin nôkwaniyiw
awa *Sapp* otâpasinahikêwinihk

êkâ ta-kî-ânwêhtamihk iyikohk ê-kistêyihtâkwaniyiki okakêskihkêmowiniwâwa ôki kêhtê-ayak. anita tâpasinahikêwinihk mîna asici kêhtê-ayak otâcimowiniwâhk kêyâpic pimohtêmakanwa kayâs nêhiyaw-kakêskimowina. êkota ôma âcimowinihk pêhtâkwan kihc-âniskotâpânak omâmitonêyihcikêwiniwâw êkwa kêyâpic êkota pimohtêmakaniyiw nêhiyaw-isîhcikêwin.

êwakon ânihi tâpasinahikana kikiskisomikonaw tânisi kâ-kî-pê-isi-itâcihocik paskwâwiyiniwak ispîhk ôta ê-kî-pa-pêyâhtakwahk pimâtisiwin. tâpwê kî-âyiman, mâka ati-kiskisiyahki kika-wâpahtênânaw iyikohk ê-miywâsiniyik onêhiyâwiwiniwâw kêyâpic kâ-sîpi-pimohtêmakaniyik kayâs ohci. *Allen Sapp* kî-miskwêyihtam tânisi ta-isi-tâpastât tâh-tâpwê nêhiyawak kâ-kî-isi-pimâcihocik, môy âyisk kî-wêhtan êkospîhk. âcimowin ôma ê-âtotamihk tâpiskôc awâsis kâ-isi-wâpahtahk. ôsisimimâw ôhi okiskisiwina kwayask ê-nôhtê-âcimot ê-tapahtêyimot. kâ-kanawâpahtaman ôhi tâpasinahikêwina kimôsihtân tânisi awa awâsis kwayask ê-isi-sîpi-kiskisit mwêhci kâ-kî-pê-isi-pimâcihot, êkosi ê-ati-nitawêyihtamahk êkota ta-ayâyahk kîstanaw.

ê-kiskisiyahk ôma kayâs-pimâtisiwin kiyânaw iyiniwak kika-kistêyimonaw ê-kihcêyihtâkwaniyik. kêhtê-ayak ôki âtotamwak ê-miywêyihtamihikocik okiskisiwiniwâwa ê-tâpasinahikâtêyiki anita tâpasinahikanihk; pa-pêyâhtak kî-kaskihtâw kâwi ta-kiskisôhât, ta-mâmitonêyihtamiyit ispîhk kâ-kî-awâsisiwiyit. âta mistahi pîkwêyihtamowin mîna pîkiskâtêyihtamowin ê-ihtakok mistahi mîna miyawâtamowin ihtakon êkwa mîna ê-mistakihtêki nêhiyaw-isîhcikêwina.

The ability to reclaim this history, to be assured that our Ancestors' ways of knowing and living have not been forgotten, allows the generation of today to build a rich future from that history. Allen's paintings bear witness to a past that held none of the distorted misperceptions and stereotypes that have led to layers of shame. Through these paintings, and with the support of the Elders, we can reconstruct an honourable history that will carry this and future generations forward with dignity. Each painting is an anchor that bridges past to present to future.

"The grandmother's role is to love my grandchildren but be able to say no."
– Bernice Simaganis

This is not merely the story of Allen Sapp; it is the story of the Nehiyawak, who are Allen Sapp's People. This is a portrayal of a simple, though difficult life lived on the Saskatchewan Prairies. As the Elders view the paintings, they are taken back to the time "where the pace was a whole lot slower than it is today" (Wallace Simaganis). Life in those days was hard work; this reality transcended cultural boundaries. Life was hard for everyone in rural areas on the Prairies in the 1930s and '40s when Allen Sapp was a youngster. The story he shares with the world is the story of a way of life steeped in the traditional values of sharing, humility, love and respect. The values that were part of Allen Sapp's happy childhood were integral to the entire community he resided in and to the people he resided with. At Dr. Gonor's urging, and with the support and encouragement of his community, Allen Sapp becomes Kiskayetum (He perceives it) and shares his childhood with the world.

ê-kaskihtâhk kâwi ta-otinamihk ôhi âcimowina êkota kayâs nêhiyaw-pimâtisiwin kâ-âtotamihk êkosi tâh-tâpwê ta-isi-kêhcinâhohk ôtê nîkân ka-ohci-wêyôtaniyik kitâniskotâpâninawak opimâtisiwiniwâw. tâpwêmakaniyiwa awa *Allen* otâpasinahikêwina môy êkota kiwâpamâw nêhiyaw ê-mac-âyiwit môy kîkway êkota ta-nêpêwihikohk. kêhtê-ayak asici ôhi tâpasinahikêwina kika-kî-kaskihtânaw ta-miywastâyahk nêhiyaw kâ-isi-âcimiht êkwa êkota ohci ôki kitâniskotâpâninawak mîna kikihc-âniskotâpâninawak ka-wîcihikwak kwayask ta-pimohtêhocik. tahto tâpasinahikan âniskêstâmakan pimâtisiwin ôtê nâway isko anohc mîna ôtê pêci-nîkân isko.

Taking His Boy for a Ride
okosisa ê-têhtapîhât

"ôhkomimâw wiya piko ta-sawêyimât ôsisima mâka mîna ta-kaskihtât 'namôya' ta-itât."
– Bernice Simaganis,
kêhtê-aya

namôya ôma *Allen Sapp* piko ê-âcimiht; mâka paskwâwi-nêhiyawak mîna ê-âcimihcik, otâyisiyinîma awa *Allen Sapp*. ê-tâpastâhk ôma ôta opimâcisiwiniwâw êkospîhk ê-kî-âyimahk mâka mîna ê-kî-pa-pêyâhtakwahk ê-wîkicik paskwâw-askîhk ôta kisiskâciwanihk. kâ-ka-kitâpahtahkik ôhi tâpasinahikana kêhtê-ayak kiskisôhikowak ispîhk "kâ-kî-ka-kâmwâtahk pimâcisiwin ispîhci anohc" *(Wallace Simaganis, kêhtê-aya)*. êkospîhk wiya pimâtisiwin mêtoni kî-sôhkatoskâniwan, môy mâka piko wiyawâw mâka pikw âwiyak mîna kî-sôhkatoskêwak. ispîhk *Allen Sapp* kâ-awâsisiwit, *1930s* isko *1940s* awasimê kâ-akimiht askiy, pikw âwiyak misiwê ôta paskwâhk kî-nayêhtâwîwak ta-pimâcihocik. êwako ôma kâ-âcimostawât ayisiyiniwa misiwêskamikohk âtotam nêhiyaw-tâpwêwakêyihtamowina: kisêwâtisiwin, tapahtêyimisowin, sâkihitowin, êkwa manâcihiwêwin. êwakon ôhi kakêskimowina wiya *Allen Sapp* ê-kî-isi-pimitisahahk asici kahkiyaw wîc-ayisiyinîma itê kâ-kî-tas-ôhpikit, ê-kî-wiyâtikosit. êkosi êkwa anihi *Gonor*a êkwa wîc-âyisiyinîma ê-sîhkimikot kî-mâci-tâpasinahikêw *Allen*, tâpwê *Kiskayetum* (kiskêyihtam) êkwa wiya ê-mâci-âcimostawât pikw âwiya misiwêskamikohk tânisi kâ-kî-pê-is-ôhpikit.

This transition is momentous. It is no longer necessary to be a good Indian painter; it is now imperative to take responsibility as a Cree painter of stories. While the early, pre-Gonor paintings are good, it is clear that Allen Sapp's true perception of the gift he was given really manifested itself in his later works. The object of his paintings comes simply from the creativity that springs from his heart and soul. His life has been lived, thus far, through his paintings and his singing and dancing and the stories he tells in his language. They are an example of the foundational philosophy of the Cree – that "in spite of the hardship, the values and beliefs, the essence of who they were has survived" (Gordon Tootoosis). It is important to note that his paintings reflect the natural changing of the seasons. Winter scenes abound because, on the harsh Saskatchewan Plains, we still experience a long stretch of bitter cold. Throughout the paintings, whether they are cold or warm, Allen Sapp has imbued them with the Cree way of living and the intrinsic connection to the land and the language. "The importance of family, community, generosity, prayer and respect … [whether visual or oral] the Cree language conveys the words and ways of seeing and knowing" (Gordon Tootoosis).

Bringing Jumping Deer Home
ê-pê-kîwêhtahât kwâskwêpayihôsa

"This was a natural way, living on the land."
– Allen Sapp

mêtoni mâmaskâtêyihtâkwan iyikohk ê-kwêskâtisit. môy êkwa piko ta-nihtâ-tâpasinahikêt iyiniw mâka sôskwâc kwêyask otâpasinahikêwiyiniw ta-tâpasinahahk nêhiyaw-âcimowina. kî-miywâsiniyiwa anihi otâpasinahikana mwayês anihi *Gonor*a ê-kiskêyimât mâka ayiwâk êkwa awa *Allen Sapp* omiyikowisiwin nôkwaniyiw mwêstas otâpasinahikêwinihk. otêhihk mîna otahcahkohk awa ohci kâ-pasikômakaniyiki otâpasinahikêwina. otâpasinahikêwina, onikamowina, onîmihitowin êkwa kâ-nêhiyawêt mâna kâ-âcimot êkota anima kâ-pimi-pimâcisit, êkota miskikâtêw nêhiyâwi-tâpwêwakêyihtamowin – "kiyâm âta ê-âyimahk anihi kâ-kistêyihtâkwahki mîna kâ-tâpwêwakêyihtamihk kêyâpic pimohtêmakaniyiw anita onêhiyâwiwiniwâhk" (*Gordon Tootoosis*). piko mîna ta-nâkatohkêhk ê-kî-tâpastât otapasinahikêwinihk kâ-kwêskâyiwaniyik.

mihcêtwâw kî-tâpastâw ê-piponiyik otâpasinahikêwinihk ayis mêtoni nayêhtâwan ôta paskwâhk êkwa kêyâpic kinwês mâna kisinâw. ê-kisinâk ahpô ê-kîsopwêyâk *Allen Sapp* kêyâpic cikêmâ misiwê otâpasinahikêwinihk tâpastâw nêhiyaw-pimâtisiwin mîna môsihtâniwan kâ-isi-manâcihtâcik askiy mîna kâ-kistêyihtahkik onêhiyawêwiniwâw. "iyikohk kâ-kistêyihtâkwahki mitêhêwâm, mâmawihtâwin, kisêwâtisiwin, kâkîsimowin, êkwa manâcihitowin, [kâ-wâpahtamihk ahpô kâ-pêhtamihk], kâ-nêhiyawêhk tâpwê mistahi itwêmakanwa tânisi kâ-isi-itâpahtamihk mîna tânisi kâ-kiskêyihtamihk" (*Gordon Tootoosis*).

"êkosi kwayask askiy kî-mosci-ohtâcihonâniwan."
– Allen Sapp

It is magical to spiral back and watch, as though we are with the painter. In one painting we become the youngster captivated as he watches *ôhkoma* bead moccasins for him. These could be the moccasins that will take him to the pow wows he loves. And, looking closely as he paints these pow wow images, we see that he has found the place where he belongs, that his spirit comes to life when he dances and sings. When he paints the pow wow he paints himself into it, so that we can watch him participate, not merely observe with him. In another painting you can feel the bitter winter wind of the Saskatchewan Prairies as the men carry out their daily duties. Their role took them outdoors, to chop the wood for the fire, to tend to the horses, and to travel and hunt. These are important reminders of a life that was harsh and difficult, where all had a role to fulfill. The hard work was not just for the men, but women and children too.

"I was old enough to snare rabbits when I was four, when I was old enough to walk in the deep snow."
– *Jonas Semaganis*

Allen Sapp was the grandson of a hard-working family, a hard-working people. Their life was not without joy. Balance was found in song and dance, prayer, laughter and play. Through his paintings we can enter into his childhood – as we enter into the Soonias kitchen, the fire is roaring and we are easily drawn into the image, standing at the shoulder of *omosôma* as he stretches the hide for a new drum. Just earlier that day the hide was stretched over the frame. The smoke is both comforting and stinging our eyes.

Blowing Snow
ê-pîwahk

tâpwê mamâhtâwan ta-nitaw-kitâpahkêhk, tâpiskôc ê-wîcêwâyahk otâpasinahikêw. anita pêyak tâpasinahikanihk tâpiskôc êkota ê-awâsisiwiyan ê-kitâpamat kôhkom ê-mîkisistahamâsk maskisina. ahpô êtikwê ôhi êwakoni ka-kikiskahk ana nâpêsis itohtêci itê kâ-miywêyihtahk kâ-pwâtisimohk. êkw êkwa kanawâpam ê-ati-tâpastât ôhi kâ-wâpahtahk anita pwâtisimowinihk, ê-miskahk ita kâ-tipêyihtâkosit, ê-pasikôyit mâna otahcahkoma kâ-nîmihitot mîna ispîhk kâ-nikamot. ispîhk mâna kâ-tâpasinahahk pwâtisimowin tâpasinahosow wîsta êkota êkosi kiyânaw ê-wîcêwâyahk ka-kanawâpamâyahk ê-nîmihitot môy piko tâpasinahikêwin ê-kanawâpahtamahk. anita mîna kotak tâpasinahikêwinihk kika-kî-môsihtân ê-tahkiyowêk ôta ôma paskwâhk kisiskâciwanihk nâpêwak ê-tasihkahkik anihi tahto kîsikâw mâna kîkwaya kâ-atoskâtahkik. êwakoni mâna katâc ta-wayawîcik ta-nitaw-nâcimihtêcik, ta-pamihastimwêcik, êkwa ta-papâmi-pimohtêhocik mîna ta-mâcîcik. mêtoni kikiskisomikon iyikohk ê-âyimahk pimâcisiwin, ê-kî-nayêhtâwahk êkosi pikw âwiyak kî-wîcihtâsow. namôya nâpêwak piko kâ-kî-sôhkatoskêcik mâka mîna iskwêwak êkwa awâsisak wîstawâw.

"ê-nêwo-piponêyân nikî-têpi-ispîhtisîn ka-nitaw-tâpakwêyân, ê-têpi-ispîhisiyân ka-pimohtêyân ê-timikonik"
– *Jonas Semaganis*, kêhtê-aya

Allen Sapp omosôma êkwa ôhkoma kî-kakâyawisîyiwa, kî-kakâyawisîwak êwakonik ayisiyiniwak. namôya mâka kahkiyaw kîkway kî-âyiman kî-miyo-pimâtisiwak mîna. kî-môcikihtâwak ê-nikamocik, ê-nîmihitocik, ê-kâkîsimocik, ê-pâhpicik êkwa ê-mêtawêcik. ôta otâpasinahikêwinihk kika-kaskihtânaw ta-wâpahtamahk tânisi kâ-kî-pê-isi-ohpikihiht – êkosi ê-ati-pîhtikwêyahk anita sôniyâsak opaminawasowikamikowâhk ê-misi-kotawêhk êkota kîstanaw ê-nîpawiyahk ê-kitâpamimâyahk omosôma ê-mêkwâ-sîpahwâyit pahkêkinwa ê-wî-osîhâyit mistikwaskihkwa. anohcihkê nawac anima pahkêkin ê-kî-taswêkipitamihk mâtahikanâhtikohk êkwa anima kâ-kaskâpahtêk kimiyomahcihikonaw pêskis ê-ohcikawâpihikoyahk.

With another painting, how easily we climb the tree and then sit in stillness and watch as the men return weary from the fields. There is a bittersweet joy as we stand, with him, at the edge of the ice watching the children play hockey. It is difficult for our hearts and minds not to be touched by such images, in knowing that the child looking on could not participate because of sickness. However, there is no self-pity evident, nor is there any of the deep sadness conveyed by other testimonials of the era of reserve life for Aboriginal Peoples.

Allen Sapp consciously, deliberately sets out to portray his people, his childhood, in such a way that we see the beauty and reality in the life of the Plains Cree in vivid clarity, with each brushstroke imbued with the facts of the moment. We see very little of the pain, heartbreak and desolation of the little boy who was in poor health, who grieved for a mother lost too soon, or for the poverty that was the reality of all who lived on the reserve. That does not diminish this reality, but builds upon the richness of the stories not often told that speak to the resilience and resistance of the Cree and other First Nations People.

These paintings project warmth, an emotional, physical, cognitive and spiritual warmth that appears in abundance in the form of his family's caring and support and his connectedness to the others in his community. In each painting we see Sapp's ability to enjoy the beauty of the land, to learn the traditional ways that will ensure his own survival as well as the survival of the future generations and, most importantly, the interwoven and naturally occurring spirituality that appears in glimpses of the ceremonies.

One of Her Grandsons
pêyak ôhi ôsisima, nâpêsisa

kotak êkwa mîna tâpasinahikêwin, mêtoni kiwêhci-iskwâhtawînaw mîtosihk êkota ê-koskowâtapiyahk nâpêwak ê-kanawâpamâyahkik ê-pê-kîwêcik kistikânihk ohci. namôya tâpwê kimiywêyihtênaw ê-wîcikâpawîstawâyahk sisonê anita miskwamîhk ê-kanawâpamât anihi awâsisa *hockey* ê-mêtawêyit. âyiman êkâ ta-kî-sîhcihikoyahk kitêhinâhk mîna kimâmitonêyihcikaninâhk ôhi tâpasinahikêwina ayis ê-kiskêyihtamahk awa awâsis êkâ wiya ê-kaskihtât ta-wîci-mêtawêmât osâm ê-nêsowâtisit. namôya mâka ahpô êkota kiwâpahtênaw kitimâkêyimisowin; nama kîkway mîna êkota pîkiskâtêyihtamowin kâ-âtotamihk mâna kâ-âcimihcik iyiniwak êkospîhk askîhkânihk kâ-kî-wîkicik.

ohcitaw awa anima *Allen Sapp* kâ-isi-tâpasinahwât wîci-nêhiyawa mîna ispîhk kâ-kî-pê-is-ôhpikit ê-awâsisiwit êkosi êkota ohci kita-kî-wâpahtamahk anima kâ-miywâsiniyik kâ-kî-isi-pimâcisiyit paskwâwi-nêhiyawa, mêtoni kwayask ê-tâpastât, tahtwâw kâ-sisopêhikêt. apisîs piko êkota tâpasinahikâtêw anima kâ-kî-wîsakitêhêt mîna kâ-kî-kîwâtisit ana nâpêsis kâ-kî-nêsowâtisit, ê-kî-wanihât okâwiya ispîhk ê-awâsisiwit, ahpô mîna anima pikw âwiya ê-kitimâkisiyit êkota askîhkânihk. namôya mâka ê-kakwê-pîwêyihtamihk anima mâka nayêstaw êkota ka-wâpahtamihk iyikohk paskwâwiyiniwak, nêhiyawak mîna kotakak iyiniwak ê-sôhkâtisicik mîna kêyâpic ê-pimowatâcik kâ-kî-isi-kakêskimihcik kayâs.

êkota tâpasinahikêwinihk wâpahcikâtêw mîna môsihtâniwan iyikohk awa otâpasinahikêw ê-kî-sawêyimikot mîna ê-kî-sîtoskâkot otêhêwâma êkwa mîna ê-kî-tipêyihtâkosit anita askîhkânihk. anita tahto tâpasinahikanihk kiwâpahtênaw iyikohk ê-miywêyihtahk êkota ê-miywâsiniyik kîkwaya, mîna kâ-isi-nôhtê-kiskêyihtahk kayâs nêhiyaw-isîhcikêwina ê-nôhtê-kêhcinâhot iyiniwak ôtê pêci-nîkân wîstawâw ta-pimitisahahkik ôhi nêhiyaw-isîhcikêwina êkwa mîna nawac anima kâ-ahcahkowahk, kâ-mamâhtâwahk ta-kiskêyihtahkik.

The warmth of family and of "All My Relations" settles upon us like a blanket around our shoulders, or "like the moss bag … where the baby is warm in a womb" (Josephine Frank). The snugness of the mossbag, the weight and warmth of the blanket, the crackle and radiance of the fire, the snare and bounce of the new drum being made by *omosôma*, the rich smoky scent of hides and the hum of *ôhkoma* as she worked – all are so very tangible. These images, poignant and lovely, are reminders to us all that these ways were real. This is the way of life that allowed for a whole child to emerge and enter the world, despite its sometime cruelty and confusion – a child who carried in his heart the values of truth, humility, love and respect, for self and others and for all living things.

Going to a Christmas Party
manitowi-kîsikâw môcikihtâwin ê-itohtêcik

When Allen Sapp speaks and describes his work, we can hear the lessons he was taught. His work, as he says, is his way of keeping those old ways alive so others can see them and, hopefully, experience a little of what it was like. "I put it down so it doesn't get lost and people will be able to see and remember" (Allen Sapp). These are important lessons that must not be forgotten.

"Portrayed in those pictures…[is] something that was rich within our lives that made it vital to our well-being."
– *Jonas Semaganis*

sawêyimitowin mitêhêwâmihk mîna "kahkiyaw niwâhkômâkanak" ohci kitakwanahikonaw tâpiskôc akohp ahpô cî "tâpiskôc wâspison … ita kâ-kîsôsit oskawâsis mêkwâc iskwêw kâ-kikiskawâwasot" (*Josephine Frank*, kêhtê-aya). kâ-sîhtwahpitêk anima wâspison, iyikohk anima akohp kâ-kîsowâk, mîna anima kâ-pahkitêk ê-wâstêpayik iskotêw, kâ-nahihtâkosiyit anihi oski-mistikwaskihkwa kâ-mêkwâ-osîhâyit omosôma, ê-kîhkâmâkwahk pahkêkin, êkwa mîna ê-tasi-nikamosisiyit ôhkoma kâ-mêkwâ-atoskêyit – kahkiyaw ôhi tâpiskôc tâh-tâpwê êkota ê-ay-ispayik. mêtoni êkota kâ-tâpasinahikâtêki anihi kâ-miywâsiki mîna kâ-kitimâkahki kikiskisomikonânaw tâpwê êkosi ê-kî-ispayik, êkosi ôma ê-kî-pê-isi-pimâcihohk êkota awâsis ê-kî-isi-pakitinikowisit âta âskaw ka-wâpahtahk kîkway kâ-mâyâtaniyik – êkota awa awâsis otêhihk ê-pê-tâpwêwakêyihtahk – tâpwêwin, tapahtêyimisowin, sâkihitowin, manâcihitowin, ka-kihcêyimisot mîna kahkiyaw awiya ka-kihcêyimât êkwa mîna kotaka kâ-pimâtahki ka-kihcêyihtahk.

ispîhk mâna awa *Allen Sapp* kâ-pîkiskwâtahk ka-kî-pêhtênaw ê-kî-nahihtahk kâ-kakêskimikot okêhtê-ayima. êkota anima otâpasinahikêwinihk ê-kanawêyihtahk, ê-âsônamawât ayisiyiniwa êkosi wîstawâw apisîs ta-kiskêyihtahkik tânisi ê-kî-pê-isi-pimâcihohk itwêw. "nitâpastân êkosi êkâ ta-wanihtâhk êkwa mîna iyiniwak ta-wâpahtahkik, ta-kiskisicik" (*Allen Sapp*). mêton ôhi kakêskimowina ê-kistêyihtâkwahki êkwa êkâ kita-kî-wanikiskisihk.

"êkota anima ê-tâpastêk kîkway kâ-kî-wêyôtahk kipimâtisiwininâhk, kîkway kâ-kî-wîcihikoyahk ta-miyw-âyâyâhk."
– *Jonas Semaganis*, kêhtê-aya

It is through sharing his stories that Sapp honours all of his People with the gift of his memories of the Plains Cree. The paintings depict a life of simple abundance and the comforts of a young boy whose life was a gift from the Creator, a boy who understood the meaning of respect for all living things and who was able to appreciate and "accept their own little space in this vast creation" (Wallace Simaganis). This young life was nurtured and encircled with the caring and love of a community whose way of life was to ensure the survival of all, the care of all, the love of all. There is no one outside of this circle, and by sharing his paintings, his life, Kiskayetum generously invites us all to enter into the circle to share the experiences that allowed him to be simply Allen Sapp and share the gifts given to him as Kiskayetum (He perceives it). This is a healing journey. It speaks to the important message the Elders are reminded of when looking at these images. As we continue to find ways to connect past to future, we honour our own responsibilities to protect and nurture our culture and to share both the burdens and the joys. To do so is, as Kiskayetum so beautifully models, to ensure the survival of all of our future generations.

"If you don't believe how can you have faith in yourself, in your capabilities, in that there's faith, strength …"
    – *Wallace Simaganis*

Quillwork Medallion
wâwiyêstahikan ê-pîmikitêhamihk

kistêyihtâkohêw kahkiyaw otayisiyinîma ê-âtotahk tânisi ê-isi-kiskisitotawât paskwâwi-nêhiyawa. êkota otâpasinahikêwinihk nôkwaniyiw pimâcisiwin ê-wêyôtahk mîna ê-pa-pêyâhtakwahk êkota oski-oskinîkîs ê-kî-pakitinikowisit, ê-kî-kiskêyihtahk kahkiyaw kîkway ta-kistêyihtahk, "ê-kî-otinahk anima anita kâ-kî-miyikowisicik wiyawâw …" (*Wallace Simaganis,* kêhtê-aya) êkota anima otayisiyinînâhk ê-kî-sawêyimiht, ê-kî-sîtoskâht, ê-kî-sîtoskâtitocik isa piko ayis êkosi piko ka-kî-isi-pimâcihocik. nam âwiyak âtawêyimâw êkota, êkwa kiskêyihtam kiwîsâmikonaw êkota ta-pîhtokwêyahk tâ-kiskêyihtamahk kîstanaw tânisi *Allen Sapp* kâ-kî-pê-isi-pimâcisit êkwa mîna ta-wâpahtamahk kiskêyihtam kâ-kî-isi-miyikowisit. pimohtêhowin ôma ta-nanâtawihisohk. êwak ôma kâ-isi-kiskisomikocik kêhtê-ayak mâna kâ-kitâpahtahkik ôhi tâpasinahikêwina. piko kapê ta-kakwê-miskamihk tânisi ta-isi-âniskotastâhk ôta anihi nâway kâ-kî-pê-itâcihohk, kika-kistêyihtênânaw iyikohk ê-aspêyimotikawiyahk ta-kanawêyihtamahk mîna ta-kiskinohamâkêyahk kinêhiyâwiwininaw êkwa mîna ta-wîcihtâsoyahk mîna ta-miyawâtamahk. pêyakwan tâpiskôc kiskêyihtam kâ-itôtahk, kâ-âsônamâkêhk, ta-kêhcinahohk ôtê nîkânihk kitâniskotâpâninawak onêhiyâwiwiniwâw ta-pimitisahahkik êwako ta-pimowâtâcik wîstawâw.

"kîspin namôya kîkway kitâpwêwakêyihtên tânisi kîkway kê-isi-pimohtêhikoyan kâ-kî-pakitinikowisiyan ka-âpacihtâyan kîkway kâ-kî-miyikowisiyan êkota ohtinikâniwan tâpwêwakêyihtamowin, sôhkisiwin, sôhkêyihtamowin"
    – *Wallace Simaganis,* kêhtê-aya

Through the Eyes of the Cree

– *L. Whiteman and L. Carrier*

"It's good to know things like that are not forgotten."
– *Irene Fineday*

The paintings of Allen Sapp tell many stories. These paintings are a veritable journey into the memory of their creator. The Plains Cree traditional way of life resonates as though from the skin of a beautiful handmade drum. Allen Sapp, Kiskayetum (*kiskêyihtam*, He perceives it) shares warmly and freely of the gifts he was given; to portray his childhood experiences growing up in the 1930s and '40s on the harsh Saskatchewan Prairies. Stories spring from canvas. Memories dance in pure colour. Kiskayetum's life has been an array of experiences that he has painted with a palette that is full, not just with colours but with his own emotions. These emotions saturate each canvas with the joy, sorrow, gratitude, responsibility, love, respect and deep humility that define not only him but the values he has been entrusted to convey to future generations. He honours his role and responsibility as he carries on the oral tradition of his people. His gift as a storyteller utilizes images, not words, that remind the Elders of the importance of identity and cultural values. These values are intended for Sapp, as a grandson, and for his grandchildren and for theirs and so on. He explains, "I can't write a story or tell one in the white man's language so I tell what I want to say with my painting."

À travers les regards des Cris

– *L. Whiteman et L. Carrier*

"C'est bien de savoir que des choses comme ça ne sont pas oubliées."
– *Irene Fineday*

Les tableaux d'Allen Sapp racontent beaucoup d'histoires. Ces tableaux sont un véritable voyage dans la mémoire de leur créateur. Le mode de vie traditionnel des Cris des Plaines résonne comme la peau d'un beau tambour fait à la main. Allan Sapp, Kiskayetum (*kiskêyihtam*, Il le perçoit) partage généreusement et chaleureusement les talents qu'il a reçus : illustrer les expériences de son enfance dans les années 1930 et 1940 dans les Prairies hostiles de la Saskatchewan. Les histoires jaillissent de la toile. Les souvenirs dansent dans une pureté de couleurs. La vie de Kiskayetum a été une série d'expériences qu'il a peintes avec une palette riche non seulement en couleurs mais aussi en émotions personnelles. Ces émotions imprègnent chaque toile de joie, de tristesse, de gratitude, de responsabilité, d'amour, de respect et d'une profonde humilité qui non seulement le définissent mais qui caractérisent aussi les valeurs qu'on lui a confiées pour qu'il les transmettent aux générations futures. Il fait honneur à son rôle et à sa responsabilité en poursuivant la tradition orale de son peuple. Son don de conteur s'appuie sur des images et non des mots, des images qui rappellent aux Aînés l'importance de l'identité et des valeurs culturelles. Ces valeurs sont destinées à Allen Sapp, en tant que petit-fils, et à ses petits-enfants et aux leurs et ainsi de suite. Il explique : "Je ne peux pas écrire une histoire ou en raconter une dans la langue de l'homme blanc alors je raconte ce que je veux dire avec ma peinture."

Pow Wow (1989)
Pow-wow (1989)

Indeed, the Creator has given Allen Sapp a special gift to paint pictures, but what is truly wondrous is his capacity to imbue these pictures in such a way as to stir the memories of the Elders. When the Elders look at these paintings they see and remember their past. As they are drawn back, with some sentimental nostalgia, the Elders begin to reconnect memory with the time and space where they grew up. In the process of recollection begins an important connection that fuses our present to the past and to the ancient generations of long ago.

The importance of Allen Sapp's work cannot be appreciated by seeing it simply as a collection of beautiful paintings. Equally important to note is the effect that these pictures have on the old people, particularly the Cree Elders. Look at these paintings through the eyes of their creator and you will learn of the world through the eyes of the Cree. Lessons about living in the harsh climate abound as the Elders look at Sapp's paintings and remember. Remembering is paramount to learning, especially when the lessons have been all but forgotten in our collective memories because of the circumstances of colonization. Remembering is resistance. When our Elders are stirred at these pictures of the recent past, they help young people learn about the shooting of rabbits; making dry meat (*kahkêwakwa*); how to make fish baskets; the way the stick has to be grooved out so the rope won't slide; how to find Seneca root (*mînisîhkês*) and other medicines and how and when to use them; to understand the importance of ceremonies, the prayers and the songs; the trees that were best for the tipi poles; the connection to the land; the connection to animals and to all living things.

Looking at My Grandmother's Grave from the Other Side
Regardant la tombe de ma grand-mère de l'autre côté

C'est vrai que le Créateur a donné à Allen Sapp un don spécial pour peindre des tableaux mais, ce qui est vraiment merveilleux, c'est sa capacité de le faire d'une manière qui ravive les souvenirs des Aînés. Quand les Aînés regardent ces tableaux, ils voient leur passé et s'en souviennent. En repensant au passé avec une nostalgie sentimentale, les Aînés commencent à rétablir le lien entre leur mémoire et l'époque et l'endroit dans lesquels ils ont grandi. Dans ce processus de souvenir, il s'établit une relation importante qui fait fusionner notre présent avec le passé et avec les anciennes générations d'il y a longtemps.

On ne peut apprécier l'importance de l'œuvre d'Allen Sapp si on la voie simplement comme une collection de beaux tableaux. Il est tout aussi important de noter l'effet de ces toiles sur les personnes âgées, en particulier les Aînés cris. Regardez ces toiles avec les yeux de leur créateur et vous connaîtrez le monde à travers les regards des Cris. Lorsque les Aînés regardent les peintures de Sapp et se souviennent, les leçons abondent sur la vie dans un climat hostile. Se souvenir est primordial pour apprendre, surtout lorsque les leçons ont été presque complètement oubliées dans nos souvenirs collectifs à cause des circonstances de la colonisation. Se souvenir c'est résister. Lorsque nos Aînés sont amenés à se souvenir, comme ils le font si facilement en regardant des images de ce passé récent, ils aident les jeunes à apprendre comment tirer sur des lapins, comment faire sécher la viande (*kahkêwakwa*); comment faire des bourriches à poissons, comment faire une rainure dans un bâton pour que la corde ne glisse pas, comment trouver le sénéca (*mînisîhkês)* et d'autres plantes médicinales, comment les utiliser et à quel moment; à comprendre l'importance des cérémonies, des prières et des chants, les meilleurs arbres pour les perches du tipi, la relation avec la terre, les animaux et toutes les choses vivantes.

The lessons that emerge when the Elders look at the paintings are undeniably important. The paintings, combined with the Elders' stories, represent a framework of important traditional Cree teachings that have survived through the generations. In this survival story beats the heart of the Ancestors and within it flickers the hopeful flame of a culture that is alive.

These paintings take us back to a place and time when the Plains Cree had a simpler way of life. There was hardship, to be sure, but as you look back you can experience the beauty of a culture that has withstood the changes of the seasons and the changes of the times. Allen Sapp has found a way to portray the way of life of the Cree people, without oversimplifying or romanticizing.

This story is told through a child's eyes. These are the memories of a grandson whose heartfelt desire is to tell the story with honesty and humility. You feel the child's sense of vulnerability as he so accurately captures and depicts the details of his daily life, so much so that an undercurrent of longing for that moment builds within us.

Recapturing this past allows us, as First Nations People, to feel the pride in what was an honourable, beautiful way of life. The Elders speak of the moments captured in his paintings with fond recollection; he has been able to gently take them by the heart back to the moments of their childhood. Despite much bitterness and sadness, there is joy in the richness of the values of the Plains Cree culture.

Les leçons qui ressortent lorsque les Aînés regardent les tableaux sont indéniablement importantes. Les peintures combinées aux histoires des Aînés représentent un cadre d'enseignements cris traditionnels importants qui ont survécu de génération en génération. Dans cette histoire de survie bat le cœur des ancêtres et, dans ce cœur brille la flamme de l'espoir d'une culture bien vivante.

Ces tableaux nous ramènent à une époque où la vie des Cris des Plaines était plus simple. Bien sûr, il y avait la misère, mais en remontant le temps, vous verrez la beauté d'une culture qui a résisté aux changements des saisons et aux changements d'époques. Allen Sapp a trouvé un moyen de représenter la vie du peuple cri sans trop la simplifier ou la romancer.

Cette histoire nous est racontée à travers le regard d'un enfant. Ce sont les souvenirs d'un petit-fils dont le désir le plus cher est de raconter cette histoire avec honnêteté et humilité. On ressent la vulnérabilité de l'enfant alors qu'il saisit et représente avec tant de précision les détails de sa vie quotidienne, tant et si bien que nous ressentons une envie sous-jacente de revivre ce passé, un désir ardent de revivre ce moment.

Retrouver ce passé nous permet, en tant que peuple des Premières nations, d'être fiers de ce beau mode de vie honorable.

Chasing Gophers
Poursuivant des gauphres

Les Aînés parlent de moments saisis dans les tableaux de Sapp qui leur rappellent de bons souvenirs; il a réussi à les ramener doucement par les sentiments pour leur faire revivre des moments de leur enfance. En dépit de beaucoup d'amertume et de tristesse, il y a de la joie dans la richesse des valeurs de la culture des Cris des Plaines.

The ability to reclaim this history, to be assured that our Ancestors' ways of knowing and living have not been forgotten, allows the generation of today to build a rich future from that history. Allen's paintings bear witness to a past that held none of the distorted misperceptions and stereotypes that have led to layers of shame. Through these paintings, and with the support of the Elders, we can reconstruct an honourable history that will carry this and future generations forward with dignity. Each painting is an anchor that bridges past to present to future.

"The grandmother's role is to love her grandchildren but be able to say no."
– *Bernice Simaganis*

This is not merely the story of Allen Sapp; it is the story of the Nehiyawak, who are Allen Sapp's People. This is a portrayal of a simple, though difficult life lived on the Saskatchewan Prairies. As the Elders view the paintings, they are taken back to the time "where the pace was a whole lot slower than it is today" (Wallace Simaganis). Life in those days was hard work; this reality transcended cultural boundaries. Life was hard for everyone in rural areas on the Prairies in the 1930s and '40s when Allen Sapp was a youngster. The story he shares with the world is the story of a way of life steeped in the traditional values of sharing, humility, love and respect. The values that were part of Allen Sapp's happy childhood were integral to the entire community he resided in and to the people he resided with. At Dr. Gonor's urging, and with the support and encouragement of his community, Allen Sapp becomes Kiskayetum (He perceives it) and shares his childhood with the world.

Making a Rope for the Horse
Fabriquant une corde pour le cheval

Le besoin de reconquérir cette histoire, de s'assurer que les connaissances et la façon de vivre de nos ancêtres ne seront pas oubliées, permet à la génération d'aujourd'hui de bâtir un avenir riche à partir du passé. Les toiles d'Allen témoignent d'un passé sans les perceptions erronées et les stéréotypes qui ont abouti à des couches successives de honte. Grâce à ces tableaux et avec l'appui des Aînés, nous pouvons reconstituer une histoire honorable qui permettra à la génération actuelle et aux générations à venir d'aller de l'avant avec dignité. Chaque peinture est un point d'ancrage qui relie le passé au présent et le présent à l'avenir.

"Le rôle de la grand-mère est d'aimer ses petits-enfants mais de pouvoir dire non."
– *Bernice Simaganis*

Ce n'est pas seulement l'histoire d'Allen Sapp; C'est l'histoire de Nehiyawak, le peuple d'Allen Sapp. C'est la représentation d'une vie simple mais difficile passée dans les Prairies de la Saskatchewan. Lorsque les Aînés regardent ces tableaux, ils se souviennent de l'époque "où le rythme de vie était bien plus lent qu'aujourd'hui" (Wallace Simaganis). En ce temps-là, la vie n'était pas facile, cette réalité transcendait les frontières culturelles. La vie était dure pour tout le monde dans les années 1930 et 1940 lorsqu'Allen Sapp était jeune. L'histoire qu'il partage avec le monde est l'histoire d'un mode de vie imprégné des valeurs traditionnelles : partage, humilité, amour et respect. Ces valeurs de l'enfance heureuse d'Allen Sapp étaient une partie intégrante de la communauté au sein de laquelle il vivait et des gens avec qui il vivait. Sur les conseils pressants du Dr Gonor et avec le soutien et les encouragements de sa communauté, Allen Sapp devient Kiskayetum (Il le perçoit) et il partage son enfance avec le monde.

This transition is momentous. It is no longer necessary to be a good Indian painter; it is now imperative to take responsibility as a Cree painter of stories. While the early, pre-Gonor paintings are good, it is clear that Allen Sapp's true perception of the gift he was given really manifested itself in his later works. The object of his paintings comes simply from the creativity that springs from his heart and soul. His life has been lived, thus far, through his paintings and his singing and dancing and the stories he tells in his language. They are an example of the foundational philosophy of the Cree – that "in spite of the hardship, the values and beliefs, the essence of who they were has survived" (Gordon Tootoosis). It is important to note that his paintings reflect the natural changing of the seasons. Winter scenes abound because, on the harsh Saskatchewan Plains, we still experience a long stretch of bitter cold. Throughout the paintings, whether they are cold or warm, Allen Sapp has imbued them with the Cree way of living and the intrinsic connection to the land and the language. "The importance of family, community, generosity, prayer and respect … [whether visual or oral] the Cree language conveys the words and ways of seeing and knowing" (Gordon Tootoosis).

"This was a natural way, living on the land."
– Allen Sapp

Just Finished Feeding the Horse
Venant juste de finir de donner à manger au cheval

Cette transition est capitale. Il n'est plus nécessaire d'être un bon peintre autochtone; il faut maintenant assumer la responsabilité d'être un peintre cri qui peint des histoires. Même si les tableaux de la période d'avant Gonor sont bons, il est clair que la vraie perception par Allen Sapp du don qu'il avait reçu ne s'est vraiment manifestée que dans ses œuvres plus tardives. L'objet de ses œuvres vient simplement de la créativité qui jaillit de son cœur et de son âme. Il a passé sa vie jusque-là à travers ses tableaux, ses chants, ses danses et ses histoires qu'il raconte dans sa langue, un exemple de la philosophie fondamentale des Cris – "qu'en dépit de la misère, les valeurs et les croyances, l'essence de ce qu'ils étaient a survécu" (Gordon Tootoosis). Il est important de noter que ses toiles reflètent le changement naturel des saisons. Les scènes d'hiver abondent car dans les Plaines hostiles de la Saskatchewan nous continuons à vivre une longue période de froid glacial. Dans les scènes qu'il peint, qu'elles soient imprégnées de chaleur ou de froid, Allen Sapp insuffle le mode de vie des Cris et le lien intrinsèque à la terre et à la langue. "L'importance de la famille, de la communauté, de la générosité, de la prière et du respect … [qu'elle soit visuelle ou orale] la langue cri porte en elle les mots et les moyens de voir et de savoir" (Gordon Tootoosis).

"C'était une manière naturelle, vivre sur la terre."
– Allen Sapp

It is magical to spiral back and watch, as though we are with the painter. In one painting we become the youngster captivated as he watches *ôhkoma* bead moccasins for him. These could be the moccasins that will take him to the pow wows he loves. And, looking closely as he paints these pow wow images, we see that he has found the place where he belongs, that his spirit comes to life when he dances and sings. When he paints the pow wow he paints himself into it, so that we can watch him participate, not merely observe with him. In another painting you can feel the bitter winter wind of the Saskatchewan Prairies as the men carry out their daily duties. Their role took them outdoors, to chop the wood for the fire, to tend to the horses, and to travel and hunt. These are important reminders of a life that was harsh and difficult, where all had a role to fulfill. The hard work was not just for the men, but women and children too.

"I was old enough to snare rabbits when I was four, when I was old enough to walk in the deep snow."
– Jonas Semaganis

Allen Sapp was the grandson of a hard-working family, a hard-working people. Their life was not without joy. Balance was found in song and dance, prayer, laughter and play. Through his paintings we can enter into his childhood – as we enter into the Soonias kitchen, the fire is roaring and we are easily drawn into the image, standing at the shoulder of *omosôma* as he stretches the hide for a new drum. Just earlier that day the hide was stretched over the frame. The smoke is both comforting and stinging our eyes.

Indoor Pow Wow at Sweetgrass Reserve a Long Time Ago
Pow-wow en salle à la réserve Sweetgrass il y a longtemps

C'est magique de remonter le temps et de regarder, comme si nous étions en compagnie du peintre. Dans un tableau, nous devenons l'enfant qui regarde avec fascination *ôhkoma* qui brode des perles sur des mocassins qui lui sont destinés. Ce seront peut-être ceux qu'il portera aux pow-wows qu'il adore. Et observez bien quand il peint ces tableaux de pow-wows: il a trouvé l'endroit où il se sent chez lui, son esprit s'anime lorsqu'il danse et qu'il chante. Quand il peint le pow-wow, il se peint dans la scène pour qu'on puisse le voir participer et pas seulement observer la scène avec lui. Dans un autre tableau, vous ressentez le vent glacial de l'hiver dans les Prairies de la Saskatchewan alors que hommes vaquent à leurs tâches quotidiennes. Leur rôle était d'aller dehors, de couper du bois pour le feu, de s'occuper des chevaux, de voyager et de chasser. Ce sont des rappels importants d'une vie rude et difficile où chacun avait un rôle à jouer. Le rude labeur n'était pas seulement la responsabilité des hommes mais aussi celle des femmes et des enfants.

"J'étais assez grand pour prendre des lapins au piège, quand j'avais quatre ans, quand j'étais assez grand pour marcher dans la neige profonde."
– Jonas Semaganis

Sapp était le petit-fils d'une famille travailleuse, d'un peuple travailleur. Leur vie n'était pas sans joie. Ils trouvaient un équilibre dans le chant et la danse, la prière, le rire et le jeu. Entrez dans la cuisine des Soonias: le feu ronfle et nous entrons facilement dans l'image, il est debout derrière l'épaule de *omosôma* qui étire une peau pour un nouveau tambour. Un peu plus tôt ce jour-là, la peau a été tendue sur le cadre. La fumée est réconfortante et pique les yeux aussi.

With another painting, how easily we climb the tree and then sit in stillness and watch as the men return weary from the fields. There is a bittersweet joy as we stand, with him, at the edge of the ice watching the children play hockey. It is difficult for our hearts and minds not to be touched by such images, in knowing that the child looking on could not participate because of sickness. However, there is no self-pity evident, nor is there any of the deep sadness conveyed by other testimonials of the era of reserve life for Aboriginal Peoples.

Allen Sapp consciously, deliberately sets out to portray his people, his childhood, in such a way that we see the beauty and reality in the life of the Plains Cree in vivid clarity, with each brushstroke imbued with the facts of the moment. We see very little of the pain, heartbreak and desolation of the little boy who was in poor health, who grieved for a mother lost too soon, or for the poverty that was the reality of all who lived on the reserve. That does not diminish this reality, but builds upon the richness of the stories not often told that speak to the resilience and resistance of the Cree and other First Nations People.

These paintings project warmth, an emotional, physical, cognitive and spiritual warmth that appears in abundance in the form of his family's caring and support and his connectedness to the others in his community. In each painting we see Sapp's ability to enjoy the beauty of the land, to learn the traditional ways that will ensure his own survival as well as the survival of the future generations and, most importantly, the interwoven and naturally occurring spirituality that appears in glimpses of the ceremonies.

Man is Having Lunch
L'homme est train de déjeuner

Avec un autre tableau, avec quelle facilité nous grimpons dans l'arbre et nous restons assis sans bouger pour regarder les hommes rentrer fatigués des champs. Nous ressentons une joie teintée d'amertume en nous tenant debout près de lui au bord de la glace pour regarder les enfants jouer au hockey. Il est difficile de ne pas être touché dans notre cœur et dans notre âme par de telles images lorsqu'on sait que l'enfant qui observe ne pouvait se joindre aux autres à cause de sa maladie. Il n'y a cependant pas d'apitoiement sur soi-même ou de tristesse profonde que l'on trouve dans d'autres témoignages sur l'époque de la vie à la réserve pour les Autochtones.

Allen Sapp cherche consciemment et délibérément à peindre son peuple, son enfance d'une façon telle que nous puissions voir la beauté et la réalité de la vie des Cris des Plaines, avec une précision frappante, chaque touche du pinceau imprégnée des faits du moment. Nous y voyons très peu de la souffrance, de la peine, de l'affliction du petit garçon en mauvaise santé qui pleure sa mère trop tôt disparue ou de la pauvreté qui était la réalité de tous ceux qui vivaient à la réserve. Ce n'est pas pour diminuer cette réalité mais pour ajouter à la richesse des histoires peu souvent évoquées qui montrent la faculté de récupération et la résistance des Cris et d'autres peuples des Premières nations.

Ces peintures projettent une chaleur, une chaleur émotionnelle, physique, cognitive et spirituelle qui est abondamment présente sous la forme de l'affection et du soutien de sa famille, et de son lien avec les autres membres de sa communauté. Dans chaque toile, nous percevons sa capacité d'apprécier la beauté de la terre, d'apprendre la façon traditionnelle de faire les choses qui assureront sa survie et celles des générations à venir, et surtout, nous entrevoyons un bref instant dans les cérémonies une spiritualité spontanée sous-jacente.

The warmth of family and of "All My Relations" settles upon us like a blanket around our shoulders, or "like the moss bag … where the baby is warm in a womb" (Josephine Frank). The snugness of the mossbag, the weight and warmth of the blanket, the crackle and radiance of the fire, the snare and bounce of the new drum being made by *omosôma*, the rich smoky scent of hides and the hum of *ôhkoma* as she worked – all are so very tangible. These images, poignant and lovely, are reminders to us all that these ways were real. This is the way of life that allowed for a whole child to emerge and enter the world, despite its sometime cruelty and confusion – a child who carried in his heart the values of truth, humility, love and respect, for self and others and for all living things.

When Allen Sapp speaks and describes his work, we can hear the lessons he was taught. His work, as he says, is his way of keeping those old ways alive so others can see them and, hopefully, experience a little of what it was like. "I put it down so it doesn't get lost and people will be able to see and remember" (Allen Sapp). These are important lessons that must not be forgotten.

"Portrayed in those pictures … [is] something that was rich within our lives that made it vital to our well-being."
– *Jonas Semaganis*

Playing with a Toy
Jouant avec un jouet

La chaleur de la famille "et de toute ma parenté" nous enveloppe comme une couverture posée sur nos épaules, ou "comme le sac de mousse … où le bébé a chaud comme dans le ventre de sa mère" (Josephine Frank). Le confort douillet du sac de mousse, le poids et la chaleur de la couverture, le crépitement et l'éclat du feu, le timbre et le rebond du nouveau tambour confectionné par *omosôma*, la riche odeur de fumée des peaux et le chantonnement de *ôhkoma* qui travaille – tout cela est très tangible. Les images, poignantes et charmantes rappellent à tous que cette vie d'antan a existé, c'est le mode de vie qui a vu un enfant complet naître et arriver dans un monde parfois rempli de cruauté et de confusion – un enfant qui portait dans son cœur des valeurs – vérité, humilité, amour, respect de lui-même et des autres, et de toute chose vivante. Quand Allen Sapp parle de son œuvre et qu'il la décrit, on peut entendre les leçons qui lui ont été enseignées. Son œuvre, comme il le dit lui-même, est sa façon à lui de garder bien vivante la vie d'antan pour que d'autres puissent voir et peut-être ressentir un peu ce que c'était. "Je peins tout ça pour que ça ne se perde pas et pour que les gens puissent voir et se souvenir" (Allen Sapp). Ce sont des leçons importantes qu'il ne faut pas oublier.

"Dans ces tableaux … [il y a] quelque chose de riche au sein de nos vies qui était vital pour notre bien-être."
– *Jonas Semaganis*

It is through sharing his stories that Sapp honours all of his People with the gift of his memories of the Plains Cree. The paintings depict a life of simple abundance and the comforts of a young boy whose life was a gift from the Creator, a boy who understood the meaning of respect for all living things and who was able to appreciate and "accept their own little space in this vast creation" (Wallace Simaganis). This young life was nurtured and encircled with the caring and love of a community whose way of life was to ensure the survival of all, the care of all, the love of all. There is no one outside of this circle, and by sharing his paintings, his life, Kiskayetum generously invites us all to enter into the circle to share the experiences that allowed him to be simply Allen Sapp and share the gifts given to him as Kiskayetum (He perceives it). This is a healing journey. It speaks to the important message the Elders are reminded of when looking at these images. As we continue to find ways to connect past to future, we honour our own responsibilities to protect and nurture our culture and to share both the burdens and the joys. To do so is, as Kiskayetum so beautifully models, to ensure the survival of all of our future generations.

"If you don't believe how can you have faith in yourself, in your capabilities, in that there's faith, strength …"
— *Wallace Simaganis*

Making Beadwork
Faisant des motifs perlés

C'est en partageant ses histoires qu'Allen Sapp rend honneur à tous les membres de son peuple auquel il fait don de ses souvenirs des Cris des Plaines. Les peintures décrivent une vie de simple abondance et le bien-être d'un petit garçon dont la vie était un don du Créateur, un petit garçon qui comprenait ce qu'était le respect de toute chose vivante et qui était capable d'apprécier et "d'accepter son propre petit espace dans cette vaste création" (Wallace Simaganis). Cette jeune vie a été entourée de tendresse et d'amour par une communauté dont le mode de vie avait pour but d'assurer la survie de tous, l'affection de tous et l'amour de tous. Il n'y a personne en dehors de ce cercle et en partageant ses toiles et sa vie, Kiskayetum nous invite tous, avec générosité, à pénétrer dans ce cercle pour partager d'une part les expériences qui lui ont permis d'être tout simplement Allen Sapp et, d'autre part, les dons qu'il a reçus lorsqu'il est devenu Kiskayetum (Il le perçoit). Il s'agit d'un parcours de guérison. Il évoque l'important message dont les Aînés se souviennent lorsqu'ils regardent ces images. Alors que nous continuons à trouver des moyens de relier le passé à l'avenir, nous honorons nos propres responsabilités qui sont de protéger et de soutenir notre culture, de partager nos fardeaux et nos joies. Comme Kiskayetum en donne si bien l'exemple, agir de la sorte assure la survie de toutes nos futures générations.

"Si vous ne croyez pas, comment pouvez-vous avoir foi en vous, en vos capacités, en ça il y a foi, il y a force …"
— *Wallace Simaganis*

Beyond the Eyes of the Cree

— *Danny Musqua, Keeseekoose First Nation Saulteaux (Anishinabe) Nation*

I see the history of my people in Allen Sapp's art. Everything I experienced as a young person, being raised in a very large family on the Keeseekoose Reserve, is depicted in his paintings. My father had sixteen children and we all had to work hard to keep food on our table. Our parents and grandparents instilled in us a deep appreciation and understanding of our traditional ways and the skills needed to survive in the new world we were faced with.

My life was intertwined with the life of my grandparents, as was Allen Sapp's, and I experienced the real down-to-earth life that the old people held on to. As I was growing up, I saw my grandparents trying to hold on to the last vestiges of the world they knew and the things they had experienced and enjoyed from their youth, like living off the land, snaring rabbits, drying meat and looking for medicines. They wanted my generation to learn our traditional ways.

My grandfather talked about the time they broke the land. In 1895, my grandfather began to farm and he got a few head of cattle. My family has been farming for 110 years, and we continue to farm. I saw the threshing machines. I saw the old log tractors. I saw the old horse-drawn ploughs with two blades. All those things I saw as I was growing up.

The discipline that was needed to succeed in farming, to adapt to the new world and the new ways, was taught to us by our old people. It was based on the traditions that existed before the newcomers arrived and the things we needed to know to survive in the world. That discipline was

Hard Work
Dur labeur

Au-delà des regards des Cris

— *Danny Musqua, Aîné de la Première nation Keeseekoose, nation Saulteaux (Anishinabe)*

Je vois l'histoire de mon peuple dans l'art d'Allen Sapp. Tout ce que j'ai vécu quand j'étais jeune, élevé dans une très grande famille à la réserve Keeseekoose, est représenté dans ses tableaux. Mon père a eu seize enfants et nous devions tous travailler dur pour qu'il y ait à manger sur la table. Nos parents et nos grands-parents nous ont inculqué une appréciation et une compréhension profondes de nos coutumes traditionnelles et les compétences nécessaires pour survivre dans ce nouveau monde auquel nous étions confrontés.

Ma vie a été liée à la vie de mes grands-parents, tout comme celle d'Allen Sapp, et j'ai vraiment connu cette vie-là à laquelle tenaient les personnes âgées. En grandissant, j'ai vu mes grands-parents qui essayaient de s'accrocher aux derniers vestiges du monde qu'ils connaissaient et aux choses qu'ils avaient vécues et appréciées dans leur jeunesse : vivre des produits de la terre, prendre les lapins au piège, faire sécher la viande et chercher des plantes médicinales. Ils voulaient que ma génération apprenne ces coutumes traditionnelles.

Mon grand-père a parlé de l'époque où la terre a été divisée. En 1895, mon grand-père a commencé à cultiver la terre et il avait quelques têtes de bétail. Ma famille pratique l'agriculture depuis 110 ans, et nous continuons à cultiver la terre. J'ai vu les batteuses. J'ai vu les vieux tracteurs pour les rondins. J'ai vu les vieilles charrues à deux lames tirées par des chevaux. J'ai vu toutes ces choses-là en grandissant.

La discipline qu'il fallait pour réussir en agriculture, pour s'adapter au nouveau monde et à ces nouvelles coutumes, ce sont nos personnes âgées qui nous l'ont enseignée. Elle était basée sur les traditions qui existaient avant l'arrivée des nouveaux venus et sur les choses que

taught to us when we learned about trapping and snaring small game. The same kind of discipline was needed by our grandfathers in order to be able to sit down quietly for hours when they were singing the songs at the pow wow, at the Sundance, or when they were playing traditional hand games. That is the discipline that we had to use to succeed in the new world.

It is so comforting to know that people will see the way it was and how we struggled to adapt from that world to this world. Survival is adapting to change, and I see the adaptation of all my people in these paintings, in the same way that the Cree had to adapt. I can hear my grandfather saying, "This is the way it was, grandson; this is how we did it," and we did change, we did adapt.

Helping his Son on a Horse
Aidant son fils à monter à cheval

We were able to adapt and go through this drastic change in lifestyle because our traditional values and beliefs prepared us and gave us strength. Because of the disciplines that we learned from the old ways, we were able to transform that old way to a new way of life.

What my grandparents taught me was that you must look to the past in order to survive in the future. You must not lose your traditions, your beliefs or your identity as you walk into the future. Allen Sapp's art is our art, it shows our lives and the changes that the Anishinabe people went through, but these changes are shown through the eyes of the Cree, through the eyes of Allen Sapp and his people. I guess we could say we all own this wonderful legacy. Allen Sapp reveals to the world who we were and what we are today and what we are going to be. I thank him for my grandfather. I thank him for my children and my grandchildren.

Meegwetch *(mîkwêc,* Thank You*)*

nous devions savoir pour survivre dans ce monde. Nous avons appris cette discipline en apprenant le trappage et le piègage du petit gibier. Il fallait le même genre de discipline à nos grands-pères pour pouvoir rester sagement assis pendant des heures quand ils chantaient des chansons au pow-wow, à la danse du soleil, ou quand ils jouaient aux jeux de mains traditionnels. C'est cette discipline que nous avions pour réussir dans ce nouveau monde.

C'est tellement réconfortant de savoir que des gens vont voir cette vie d'antan et comment nous avons lutté pour passer de notre monde à ce monde-ci. La survie c'est de s'adapter au changement, et je vois cette adaptation de tout mon peuple dans ces tableaux, de la même manière que les Cris ont dû s'adapter. J'entends encore mon grand-père dire, "C'était comme ça, mon petit-fils; c'est comme ça que nous faisions," et nous avons fini par changer, nous avons fini par nous adapter.

Nous avons pu nous adapter et subir ces changements radicaux à notre mode de vie parce que nos valeurs et nos croyances traditionnelles nous ont préparés à ça et nous en ont donné la force. Grâce aux disciplines que nous avions apprises des anciennes coutumes, nous avons pu transformer cette vie d'antan en un nouveau mode de vie.

Ce que mes grands-parents m'ont enseigné c'était qu'il fallait se tourner vers le passé pour survivre à l'avenir. Il ne faut pas perdre vos traditions, vos croyances ou votre identité en marchant vers l'avenir. L'art d'Allen Sapp est notre art, il montre nos vies et les changements que le peuple Anishinabe people a vécus, mais nous voyons ces changements à travers les regards des Cris, à travers les regards d'Allen Sapp et de son peuple. Je pense que nous pouvons dire que ce legs magnifique nous appartient à tous. Allen Sapp révèle au monde qui nous étions, ce que nous sommes aujourd'hui et ce que nous deviendrons. Je le remercie au nom de mon grand-père. Je le remercie au nom de mes enfants et de mes petits-enfants.

Meegwetch *(mîkwêc,* merci*)*

The Art of Allen Sapp Tells A Story That Began Long Before His Birth
L'art d'Allen Sapp raconte une histoire qui a commencé bien avant sa naissance

Timeline Summary
Résumé chronologique

Glenbow Archives NY-1406-190

First Nations men hunting buffalo

Hommes des Premières nations chassant des bisons

iyiniwak paskwâwi-mostosa ê-nôcihâcik

Glenbow Archives

First Nations men scouting

Hommes des Premières nations allant en éclaireurs

iyiniwak ê-papâ-nâtawâpahkêcik

1640 – 1690: French fur traders and explorers first contact with the Cree.

Premiers contacts des commerçants de fourrures et des explorateurs français avec les Cris.

wêmistikôsiwak kâ-pê-nâtawâpicik êkwa kâ-pê-atâwêcik nistam kî-nakiskawêwak nêhiyawa.

1690 – 1740: Cree involved in fur trade. Served as middlemen between First Nations and English and French fur traders.

Participation des Cris au commerce des fourrures. Ils ont servi d'intermédiaires entre les Premières nations et les commerçants de fourrures anglais et français.

nêhiyawak kî-wîcihêwak ka-atâmitoyit kotaka iyiniwa êkwa mîna âkayâsiwa mîna wêmistikôsiwa.

1740 – 1780: Cree spread out westward from their original eastern homeland … across present-day provinces of Manitoba, Saskatchewan, and Alberta. Cree move south, gradually, attracted by the estimated 60 million buffalo on the North American Plains. Smallpox epidemics halted the Cree movement west.

Les Cris ont quitté leur territoire d'origine dans l'est pour aller vers l'ouest … Ils ont traversé les provinces actuelles du Manitoba, de la Saskatchewan, et de l'Alberta. Les Cris sont allés progressivement vers le sud, attirés par les soixante millions de bisons estimés dans les plaines nord-américaines. Des épidémies de petite vérole ont arrêté le mouvement des Cris vers l'ouest.

nêhiyawak sâkâstênohk kayâhtê kâ-wîkicik ohci kî-ati-papâmâcihowak nakahkpêhanohk isi … misiwê itê ôhi *Manitoba, Saskatchewan,* êkwa *Alberta* kâ-piskihtahastâhk anohc. kêtahtawê ôki nêhiyawak kî-âhcipiciwak sâwanohk isi ê-pimitisahwâcik âtiht anihi nânitaw *60,000,000* paskwâwi-mostoswa paskwâhk mihkinâhko-ministikohk. omikîwâspinêwin kî-nakinikwak nêhiyawak êkâ ayiwâk nakahkpêhanohk isi ta-itohtêcik.

1780 – 1830:

Cree alternate winter in the woodlands (north) and summer on the plains (south). Now established as buffalo-hunting people, Cree now had horses and were called Plains Cree.

Les Cris passent l'hiver dans les régions boisées (le nord) et l'été dans les plaines (le sud). Ce sont maintenant des chasseurs de bisons. Les Cris avaient des chevaux maintenant et on les appelait les Cris des Plaines.

nêhiyawak mâna kî-piponisiwak sakâhk kîwêtinohk itê mâka kî-nîpinisiwak mâna paskwâhk sâwanohk. iyiniwak kâ-nôcihâcik paskwâwi-mostoswa êkwa kî-isi-kiskêyimâwak. âtiht nêhiyawak mistatimwa kî-kâhcitinamâsowak êkwa êkota ohci paskwâwi-nêhiyawak kî-isiyihkâtâwak.

Chief Poundmaker
Le chef Poundmaker
pîhtokahânapiwiyin

Saskatchewan Archives Board

1842:

Poundmaker, Allen Sapp's grandfather's cousin, is born. Poundmaker would gain prominence as a significant chief in the 1880s.

Naissance de Poundmaker (un cousin du grand-père d'Allen Sapp). Poundmaker deviendra un chef important dans les années 1880.

nihtâwikiw pîhtokahânapiwiyin (*Allen Sapp* omosôma ociwâmiyiwa). pîhtokahânapiwiyin okimâhkân pêci-nîkân ka-kihcêyimâw ispîhk *1880s* ê-akimiht askiy.

Flying Eagle, Allen's grandfather
Flying Eagle, le grand-père d'Allen
kihiw kâ-pimihât, Allen *omosôma*

Allen Sapp Gallery Archives

1864:

Flying Eagle, Allen Sapp's grandfather, is born. He was involved in the Battle of Cut Knife Hill with Poundmaker (1885).

Naissance de Flying Eagle, le grand père d'Allen Sapp, qui a participé à la bataille de Cut Knife Hill avec Poundmaker (en 1885).

nihtâwikiw kihiw kâ-pimihât, *Allen Sapp* omosôma. wiya êkwa asici pîhtokahânapiwiyin kî-wîcihiwêwak ispîhk kâ-nôtinitohk kîskihkomânacîhk (*1885*).

Glenbow Archives

*Plains First Nations breaking land
with a plough*
*Premières nations des Plaines labourant la terre
avec une charrue*
*paskwâw-iyiniwak ê-pîkopicikêcik
pîkopicikan ê-âpacihtâcik*

Saskatchewan Archives Board

*Bones being loaded on trains
in Gull Lake, Saskatchewan*
*Chargement d'os dans des trains à Gull Lake,
en Saskatchewan*
iskotêwi-tâpânâskohk ê-pôsihtâhk oskana Gull
Lake, Saskatchewan

Saskatchewan Archives Board

Buffalo skulls stacked near Saskatoon
Crânes de bisons empilés près de Saskatoon
*ê-ahkwêtawastêki paskwâwi-mostos
mistikwânikana cîki Saskatoonihk*

Saskatchewan Archives Board

Bones in a clearing north of The Battlefords
Os dans une clairière au nord des Battlefords
*kîwêtinohk nôtinitowi-sîpîhk ohci ita
ê-paskwâsik ôhi oskana ê-astêki*

1876:   Treaty Number 6 signed at Fort Carlton between the Cree and Saulteaux, representing the First Nations, and the Dominion Government, representing the Crown.

Signature du traité numéro 6 à Fort Carlton entre les Cris et les Saulteaux, représentant les Premières nations, et le gouvernement du Dominion, représentant la Reine.

kâ-masinahikâtêk asotamâkêwin nikotwâsik pêhonânihk itê nêhiyawak asici nahkawiyiniwak, ê-nîpawîstamawâcik iyiniwa; êkwa aniki kihci-ôkimânâhk ohci ê-nîpawîstamawâcik kihc-ôkimâskwêwa.

1877:   Red Pheasant and his followers settle on a reserve near North Battleford. Today, highway signs and maps still identify this land as Red Pheasant Reserve.

Red Pheasant et ses partisans s'établissent dans une réserve près de North Battleford. Aujourd'hui, les panneaux routiers et les cartes identifient toujours cette terre comme étant la réserve Red Pheasant.

pihêw kâ-mihkosit êkwa anihi okiskinowâpamâkana nitawi-wîkiwak askîhkânihk cîki nôtinitowi-sîpîhk. anohc êkwa, kiskinowacîhtâhtikwa mîna askîwasinahikana kêyâpic anima askiy êkota mikisiwacîhk *Red Pheasant* isiyihkâtêw.

1878:   Sixty million buffalo killed in 75 years, only 1,000 remained in captivity. Cree must move to areas allotted as reserves.

Soixante millions de bisons ont été tués en soixante-quinze ans. Il en est resté seulement mille en captivité. Les Cris déménagent dans des zones attribuées comme réserves.

têpakohpomitanaw niyânanosâp askiya *60,000,000* paskwâwi-mostoswak kî-nipahâwak. kihci-mitâtahtomitanaw piko kêyâpic pimâtisiwak, mâka ê-kanawêyimihcik mênikanihk. nêhiyawak êkwa ayisâc ta-âhtokêcik ta-nitawi-wîkicik anita kâ-kî-nawasônikâtêyiki askîhkâna.

University of Manitoba Archives & Special Collections

Louis Riel
Louis Riel
Louis Riel *awa*

Glenbow Archives

*View of the battle of Cut Knife Hill
during the Riel Rebellion*
*Vue de la bataille de Cut Knife Hill
pendant la Rébellion de Riel*
*êkosi ôma ê-kî-isinâkwahk kâ-nôtinitohk anita
kîskihkomânacîhk ispîhk
kâ-mêkwâ-mâyahkamikahk*

Allen Sapp Gallery Archives

*Flying Eagle wearing war bonnet similar to the one
that was considered to have saved his life*
*Flying Eagle portant une coiffure de guerre
semblable à celle qui était considérée comme lui
ayant sauvé la vie.*
*kihiw kâ-pimihât ê-kikiskahk mikwanastotin
tâpiskôc anima kotak kâ-kî-pimâcihikot*

1885:

Uprising by Metis people led by Louis Riel. Poundmaker's people and others that were labeled hostile endure hardships due to cuts in rations by Indian Agent.
May 2: 5:00 a.m. to 12:00 noon North-West Mounted Police attacked Poundmaker's people on Poundmaker's Reserve … NWMP are forced to retreat – later to be known as the Battle of Cut Knife Hill. Flying Eagle's involvement caused him to change his name to Saposkum.

Insurrection des Métis sous la direction de Louis Riel. Le peuple de Poundmaker et d'autres qui ont été désignés comme hostiles connaissent la misère à cause des coupures de rations par l'agent des sauvages.
Le 2 mai de 5 heures du matin à midi, la police à cheval du Nord-Ouest attaque le peuple de Poundmaker à la réserve Poundmaker … La P.C.N.-O. est obligée de battre en retraite. Ce sera connu plus tard sous le nom de bataille de Cut Knife Hill. La participation de Flying Eagle l'a forcé à changer de nom et à se faire appeler Saposkum.

ê-mâyahkamikisicik âpihtawikosisânak kî-nîkânîstamâkowak pêyak *Louis Riel* kâ-kî-isiyihkâsoyit. mitoni ê-âyimisicik kî-itêyimâwak wîci-nêhiyawa mîna wiya pîhtokahânapiwiyin êkosi êwak ôhci sôniyâwikimâw apisîs kî-nakinamawêw otasahkêwiniwâw. sâkipakâwi-pîsim nîso ê-akimiht: ê-kîkisêpâyik niyânan tipahikan isko ê-âpihtâ-kîsikâyik mihkwasâkayak kî-nôcihêwak pîhtokahânapiwiyin wîci-nêhiyawa êkota kîskihkomânihk … mihkwasâkayak mâka kî-tapasîwak. mwêstas anima "kîskihkomânacîhk kâ-kî-nôtinitohk" kî-pê-isi-kiskêyihcikâtêw. ayis ê-kî-wîcihiwêt anita kâ-nôtinitohk sâposkam kî-isi-mêskotastâw owîhowin awa kihiw kâ-pimihât.

Albert Soonias
Albert Soonias
Albert Soonias *awa*

Maggie Soonias
Maggie Soonias
Maggie Soonias *awa*

Alex with his wife Agnes
Alex avec sa femme Agnes
Alex *asici owîkimâkana* Agnesa

1885: Albert Soonias, Allen Sapp's maternal grandfather, is born.

Naissance d'Albert Soonias, le grand-père maternel d'Allen Sapp.

nihtâwikiw *Albert Soonias, Allen Sapp* omosôma, okâwiya ohtâwiyiwa.

1886: Poundmaker dies at Chief Crowfoot's reserve near modern day Gleichen, Alberta.

Mort de Poundmaker à la réserve du chef Crowfoot près de Gleichen de nos jours, en Alberta.

pîhtokahânapiwiyin nakataskêw nêtê *Chief Crowfoot* otiskonikaniyiw cîki itê ôtênaw *Gleichen, Alberta* êkwa anohc kâ-isiyihkâtamihk.

1887: Maggie Soonias, Allen Sapp's maternal grandmother, is born.

Naissance de Maggie Soonias, la grand-mère maternelle d'Allen Sapp.

Maggie Soonias nihtâwikiw, *Allen Sapp* ôhkoma, okâwiya ôhi okâwiyiwa.

1901: Alex Sapp, Allen Sapp's father, is born on November 2.

Naissance d'Alex Sapp, le père d'Allen Sapp, le 2 novembre.

nîso ê-akimimiht âhkwatinowi-pîsimwa, nihtâwikiw, *Alex Sapp, Allen Sapp* ohtâwiya.

1905: Agnes Soonias, Allen Sapp's mother, is born.

Naissance d'Agnes Soonias, la mère d'Allen Sapp.

Agnes Soonias, Allen Sapp okâwiya, nihtâwikiyiwa.

1923: Alex Sapp and Agnes Soonias are married.

Mariage d'Alex Sapp et d'Agnes Soonias.

Alex Sapp êkwa *Agnes Soonias* wîkihtôwak.

Agnes holding Allen in a mossbag
Agnes portant Allen dans un sac de mousse
Agnes ê-tahkonât Allena ê-wâspisoyit

Alex and Agnes at the
Prince Albert Sanatorium
Alex et Agnes au sanatorium
de Prince Albert
Alex êkwa Agnes nêtê katôhpinêwikamikohk,
kistapinânihk

1928:

Allen Frederick Sapp (originally spelled Allan) is born on January 2 at the Red Pheasant Reserve.

Naissance d'Allen Frederick Sapp (épelé au départ Allan) le 2 janvier à la réserve Red Pheasant.

kisê-pîsim nîso ê-akimimiht, mikisiwacîhk, nihtâwikiw *Allen Frederick Sapp* (nistam *Allan* kî-itisinahikâtêyiw).

1930s:

Agnes Sapp is hospitalized intermittently, suffering from tuberculosis.

Hospitalisation de manière intermittente d'Agnes Sapp qui souffre de tuberculose.

Agnes Sapp awa nêsôwihikow anima katôhpinêwin êkosi mâna kî-âh-asiwasoyiwa katôhpinêwikamikohk.

1936:

Allen Sapp is given his Cree name, Kiskayetum (He perceives it), to ensure he would live a long and prosperous life.

Allen Sapp reçoit sont nom cri, Kiskayetum (Il le perçoit), pour lui assurer une longue vie prospère.

Allen Sapp nêhiyawi-wîhâw kiskêyihtam, ê-pakosêyimohk kinwêsk pimâtisiwin ta-ayât mîna ta-wêyôtaniyik êwako.

1930s-1940s:

The agrarian period of the Cree. Allen's formative years. His paintings depict this period.

La période agraire des Cris. Les années formatrices d'Allen. Ses tableaux représentent cette période.

êkospîhk êkwa ôma nêhiyawak kî-ati-kistikâtamwak askiy. *Allen* wîsta êkospîhk kî-kiskinohamâsow ê-kiskinowâpamât okêhtê-ayima. kahkiyaw kîkway êkospîhk kâ-kî-isi-nêhiyaw-waskawîcik otâpasinahikêwinihk tâpastêyiwa.

St. Barnabas residential school, Onion Lake
Le pensionnat St. Barnabas à Onion Lake
St. Barnabas residential school,
wîhcêkaskosîwi-sâkahikanihk

Left to right, back row: John, Allen, Alex;
front row: Henry, Simon, Stella
De gauche à droite, rangée de derrière: John,
Allen et Alex ; Rangée de devant : Henri, Simon
et Stella
namahcîhk ohci kihciniskêhk isi nâway aniki:
John, Allen, Alex; *nîkânihk aniki:* Henry, Simon
Stella

Allen on horseback
Allen à cheval
Allen *ê-têhtapit*

1941:

Allen Sapp at St. Barnabas residential school, Onion Lake, where he was very lonely and, like all students, not allowed to speak his mother tongue.

Allen Sapp est au pensionnat St. Barnabas à Onion Lake, où il se sentait très seul et, comme tous les élèves, il n'avait pas le droit de parler sa langue maternelle.

Allen Sapp awa *St. Barnabas residential school*, wîhcêkaskosîwi-sâkahikanihk ê-ayât. mistahi kî-kaskêyihtam ayis mîna kahkiyaw êkota awâsisak môy kî-pakitinâwak ta-nêhiyawêcik.

1942:

Agnes Sapp dies. Alex returns to Little Pine Reserve with all his children, except Allen. (Allen remains at the residential school.)

Mort d'Agnes Sapp. Alex retourne à la réserve Little Pine avec tous ses enfants sauf Allen. (Allen reste au pensionnat.)

Agnes Sapp nakataskêw. *Alex* kâwi nitawi-wîkiw wâskicôsihk asici kahkiyaw ocawâsimisa, namôya mâka wiya *Allen*. (*Allen* wiya wîhcêkaskosîwi-sâkahikan kiskinwahamâtowikamikohk kî-ay-ayâw.)

1947:

Allen has spinal meningitis and goes to the North Battleford Indian Hospital.

Allen a une méningite spinale et va à l'hôpital indien de North Battleford.

Allen pîhtawâwikanânâspinêw êkwa itohtahâw nôtinitowi-sîpîhk iyiniw-âhkosîwikamikohk.

1947:

Possible date of Flying Eagle's death.

Date possible de la mort de Flying Eagle.

pakahkam ôma êkospîhk ê-akimiht askiy kihiw kâ-pimihât kâ-kî-nakataskêt.

Maggie and her brother Isaac
Maggie et son frère Isaac
Maggie *êkwa wîtisâna* Isaaca

As a young man Allen participated in pow wows and traditional ceremonies
Quand il était jeune homme Allen participait à des pow-wows et à des cérémonies traditionnelles.
ê-oskinîkiwit awa Allen kî-papâ-wîcihiwêw kâ-pwâtisimohk mîna kâ-nêhiyaw-isîhcikêhk

Maggie Soonias beside Flying Eagle's war bonnet
Maggie Soonias à côté de la coiffure de guerre de Flying Eagle
Maggie Soonias *êkwa* kihiw kâ-pimihât omîkwanastotiniyiw

1948: Allen back at the Red Pheasant Reserve with his grandparents.

Retour d'Allen chez ses grands-parents à la réserve Red Pheasant.

Allen mikisiwacîhk kîhtwâm asici okêhtê-ayima.

1948-1960: Allen Sapp lives on the Red Pheasant Reserve.

Allen Sapp vit à la réserve Red Pheasant.

Allen Sapp mikisiwacîhk askîhkânihk wîkiw.

1955: Allen marries Margaret Whitford of the Little Pine Reserve. She had spent several years at the Prince Albert Sanatorium prior 1945 and, in 1957, returned for two more years during which time their son, David, was born.

Allen épouse Margaret Whitford de la réserve Little Pine. Elle avait passé plusieurs années au sanatorium de Prince Albert avant 1945 et, en 1957, elle est revenue deux années supplémentaires pendant lesquelles leur fils David est né.

Allen kihci-wîkimêw *Margaret Whitford*a wâskicôsihk ê-ohcîyit. ê-kî-asiwasoyit katôhpinêwikamikohk kistapinânihk isko *1945* êkwa kîhtwâm mîna *1957* isko *1959*. mêkwâc êkota ê-asiwasot okosisiwâwa *David* kî-nihtâwikiyiwa.

1963: Maggie Soonias, Allen's grandmother, dies.

Mort de Maggie Soonias, la grand-mère d'Allen.

Allen ôhkoma, *Maggie Soonias*, nakataskêyiwa.

Allen and his first wife, Margaret
Allen et sa première femme, Margaret
Allen *ékwa anihi nistam kâ-kî-wîwit*, Margareta

Allen painting at Hobby Shop
Allen peignant à Hobby Shop
Allen *ê-tâpasinahikêt anita* Hobby
acâwêwikamikosihk

Allen and Dr. Gonor at an exhibition
Allen et le Dr Gonor à une exposition
Allen *ékwa* Dr. Gonor *ôki ita kâ-wâpahtihiwêhk*
Allen *otâpasinahikêwina*

*Allen and Dr. Gonor with Mr. and Mrs. Eaton at
a Toronto exhibition*
*Allen et le Dr Gonor avec M. et Mme Eaton à une
exposition à Toronto*
Allen *ékwa* Dr. Gonor, *asici* Mr. *ékwa* Mrs.
Eaton *nêtê* Toronto *tâpasinahikêwina*
ê-wâpahtihiwêhk

1963:

Allen and his wife move to North Battleford. Allen works part-time at Hobby Shop, paints at home. Indian Affairs Bureau gave him a small grant. Some association with the art club, learns use of pastels and palette knife, begins to use English.

Allen et sa femme déménagent à North Battleford. Allen travaille à mi-temps à Hobby Shop et peint à la maison. Le bureau des affaires indiennes lui accorde une petite subvention. Il s'associe un peu au club d'art, apprend à se servir de pastels et d'un couteau à palette et commence à utiliser l'anglais.

Allen asici owîkimâkana âhtokêwak ê-nitaw-wîkicik nôtinitowi-sîpîhk isi. *Allen* âh-atoskêw *Hobby*-acâwêwikamikosihk, pêskis ê-tâpasinahikêt wîkihk. *Indian Affairs Bureau* kî-mosci-miyik apisîs sôniyâwa. anita kâ-mâmaw-apihtahkik tâpasinahikêwin kî-wîcihiwêw, kî-kiskinohamâsow tânisi ta-isi-âpacihtât *pastels* êkwa *palette knife*, âkayâsîmow mîna.

1966:

Allen Sapp meets Dr. Allan Gonor.

Allen Sapp rencontre le Dr Allan Gonor.

Allen Sapp nakiskawêw maskihkîwiyiniwa *Allan Gonor* ê-isiyihkâsoyit.

1967:

Allen Sapp's first exhibition, Eaton's Art Gallery, Montreal.

Première exposition d'Allen Sapp à la galerie d'art de chez Eaton, à Montréal.

Allen Sapp nistam ê-wâpahtihiwêhk otâpasinahikêwina, *Eaton's Art Gallery, Montreal.*

1969-1970:

Exhibitions in Los Angeles, New York, London.

Expositions à Los Angeles, New York, Londres.

ê-wâpahtihiwêhk otâpasinahikêwina akâmi-tipahaskânihk *Los Angeles, New York* itê, mîna *London* akâmaskîhk itê.

*Tom Hill and Allen Sapp during the filming of
Colours of Pride*

*Tom Hill et Allen Sapp pendant le tournage de
Colours of Pride*

Tom Hill *êkwa* Allen Sapp *ê-mêkwâ-
masinahipayihtâhk* Colours of Pride

*Mr. John Parkin, President of the R.C.A.A.
congratulates new member, Allen Sapp*

*M. John Parkin, président de l'ARC félicite
Allen Sapp, nouveau membre*

Mr. John Parkin, *ana kâ-nîkânapîstahk*
R.C.A.A., *ê-kistêyimât* Allena *ispîhk
kâ-pîhtokwahimiht êkota*

*Presentation by the Right Honourable Jeanne
Sauvé of the Order of Canada to Allen Sapp, on
April 29, 1987*

*Présentation par l'honorable Jeanne Sauvé
de l'Ordre du Canada à Allen Sapp,
le 29 avril 1987*

29 *ê-akimiht ayîki-pîsim, 1987,
ê-isi-kistêyimiht* Allen, *miyikow anihi*
Right Honourable Jeanne Sauvé*a anima*
Officer of the Order of Canada

1970:   National Film Board documentary. The Sapps move into a new home.

Documentaire de l'Office national du film. Les Sapp emménagent dans une nouvelle maison.

National Film Board âcikâstêpayihcikêwin âcimowin.
Sapp wiyawâw oski-wâskahikan is-âhtokêwak.

1971:   CBC documentary *By Instinct a Painter*.

Documentaire de CBC *By Instinct a Painter*.

CBC âcikâstêpayihcikêwin âcimowin *By Instinct a Painter*.

1975:   Sapp elected to Royal Canadian Academy of Arts.

Sapp est élu à l'Académie royale des arts du Canada.

Sapp pîhtokwahâw *Royal Canadian Academy of Arts*.

1985-1987:   Dr. Allan Gonor died; Allen received the Saskatchewan Order of Merit and the Order of Canada (1987).

Mort du Dr Allan Gonor; Allen reçoit le Saskatchewan Order of Merit et l'Ordre du Canada (1987).

maskihkîwiyiniw *Allan Gonor* kî-nakataskêw. *Allen* ê-kistêyimiht miyâw *The Saskatchewan Order of Merit* êkwa mîna *The Order of Canada* (1987).

Allen Sapp Gallery Archives

Allen and Mrs. Ruth Gonor
Allen et Mme Ruth Gonor
Allen *êkwa* Mrs. Ruth Gonor

Allen Sapp Gallery Archives

Allen standing in front of the public gallery bearing his name
Allen debout devant la galerie publique qui porte son nom
ê-ohtiskawikâpawit Allen *anita anima* Allen Sapp Gallery

Allen Sapp Gallery Archives

Allen and Margaret Sapp
Allen et Margaret Sapp
Allen *êkwa* Margaret Sapp

Allen Sapp Gallery Archives

Allen (right) with his father Alex Sapp (seated) and his nephews John and Melvin visiting the Allen Sapp Gallery
Allen (à droite) avec son père Alex Sapp (assis) et ses neveux John et Melvin visitant la galerie Allen Sapp
Allen *(kihciniskêhk) asici ohtâwiya* Alex Sapp *(kâ-apiyit) êkwa* Allen *otôsima* John *êkwa* Melvin *ê-pê-wâpahtamiyit* Allen Sapp Gallery

1988: Mrs. Ruth Gonor donates the Gonor Collection to the City of North Battleford.

Mme Ruth Gonor fait don de la collection Gonor à la ville de North Battleford.

Mrs. Ruth Gonor mosci-mêkiw anima *Gonor* omâwasonikêwin anita kihci-ôtênaw nôtinitowi-sîpiy ta-kanawêyihtamihk.

1989: The Allen Sapp Gallery – The Gonor Collection, opens.

Ouverture de la galerie Allen Sapp – la collection Gonor

The Allen Sapp Gallery – Gonor mâwasakonikêwin – yôhtênikâtêw

1990: Allen Sapp marries his second wife, Margaret Berryman, on June 12.

Allen Sapp épouse sa deuxième femme, Margaret Berryman, le 12 juin.

Allen Sapp mîna kîhtwâm wîkihtow, *Margaret Berryman*a ê-wêkimât, pâskâwihowi-pîsim nîsosâp ê-akimiht.

1992: Alex Sapp, Allen's father, dies.

Mort d'Alex Sapp (le père d'Allen).

nakataskêw *Alex Sapp, Allen* ohtâwiya.

1997: Saskatchewan Arts Board Lifetime Achievement Award.

Prix d'excellence pour l'œuvre de toute une vie du Saskatchewan Arts Board.

Saskatchewan Arts Board Lifetime Achievement Award Allen miyâw.

1998: Honourary Doctorate from the University of Regina

Doctorat honorifique de l'Université de Regina

Honourary Doctorate University of Regina ê-ohci-miyiht.

Allen Sapp Gallery Archives

Allen with David Bouchard at the launch of Song Within My Heart

Allen avec David Bouchard au lancement de Song Within My Heart

Allen *êkwa* David Bouchard *ispîhk nistam kâ-wâpahtamihk anima masinahikan* Song Within My Heart *(nikamowin nitêhihk)*

Allen Sapp Gallery Archives

Allen with curator Dean Bauche and M.L.A. Len Taylor at the Saskatchewan 2005 Centennial launch of the Through the Eyes of the Cree *exhibition*

Allen avec le conservateur Dean Bauche et le député provincial Len Taylor au lancement du centenaire 2005 de la Saskatchewan de l'exposition À travers les regards des Cris

Allen *asici onâkatawêyihcikêw* Dean Bauche *êkwa* M.L.A. Len Taylor *ispîhk nistam kâ-wâpahtamihk "nêhiyaw kâ-isi-wâpahtahk", anita* Centennial 2005 *ê-miyawâtamihk saskâciwanihk*

Allen Sapp Gallery Archives

Now in his mid-70s Allen still frequents the public gallery established in his name

Âgé aujourd'hui de plus de 75 ans, Allen fréquente encore la galerie publique qui porte son nom

kêkâc êkwa Allen *ayênânêwomitanaw ispihtisîw mâka kêyâpic mâna ay-itohtêw anita anima* Allen Sapp Gallery *tâpasinahikanikamikohk*

1999: National Aboriginal Lifetime Achievement Award.

Prix national d'excellence autochtone pour l'oeuvre de toute une vie.

National Aboriginal Lifetime Achievement Award miyâw.

2003: Governor General's Award for Illustration of a Children's Book by David Bouchard, *Song Within My Heart.*

Prix du Gouverneur général pour les illustrations du livre pour enfants de David Bouchard, *Song Within My Heart.*

Governor General's Award miyâw otâpasinahikêwina ohci anita awâsis masinahikanis David Bouchard kâ-kî-masinahahk, Song Within My Heart (nikamowin nitêhihk).

2005: *Through the Eyes of the Cree and Beyond* begins a national tour.

Début d'une tournée nationale de *À travers les regards des Cris et au-delà.*

"kâ-isi-wâpahtahk nêhiyaw êkwa awasimê" mâci-papâ-wâpahtihiwâniwan.

Paintings on Loan

**The following individuals and groups have generously loaned artwork from their collections.
The Allen Sapp Gallery: The Gonor Collection gratefully acknowledges their contribution
to the exhibition and catalogue, *Through the Eyes of the Cree and Beyond*.**

Allen Sapp – *Scraping a Hide*

Canadian Museum of Civilization – *Doing a Grease Job*

Native Heritage Foundation – *Practicing for the Game*

University of Lethbridge – *Inside Dance Hall at Stoney Reserve*

Private Collector – Someone Died Here
Inside My Old Home a Long Time Ago
Baby is Sleeping
Moving to a Different Place
Man in Barn
Chasing a Coyote
Blowing Snow
Cooking Supper
Cooking Potatoes

**All other paintings in the exhibition, *Through the Eyes of the Cree and Beyond*, are from the permanent
collection of the Allen Sapp Gallery: The Gonor Collection, North Battleford, Saskatchewan.**

ALLEN SAPP GALLERY
THE GONOR COLLECTION

Exhibition Venues

Allen Sapp Gallery, North Battleford, Saskatchewan

Red Deer and District Museum, Red Deer, Alberta

Western Development Museum, Saskatoon, Saskatchewan

Wanuskewin Heritage Park, Saskatoon, Saskatchewan

The Cumberland Gallery, Regina, Saskatchewan

Western Development Museum, Moose Jaw, Saskatchewan

Museum of Civilization, Hull, Quebec / Musée de la civilisation, Hull, Québec

Medicine Hat Museum, Medicine Hat, Alberta

Prince of Wales Northern Heritage Centre, Yellowknife, Northwest Territories

Swift Current Art Centre, Swift Current, Saskatchewan